Acting Edition

The Apollo Presents...
A New Harlem Renaissance

Short Plays from The New Black Fest

It's Complicated
by Michael Bradford

Thy Will Be Done
by Dennis A. Allen II

Cliff & Clara & Her Baby
by Lauren A. Whitehead

Rampjaar
by James Ijames

Color Theory
by Eric Micha Holmes

Goddess Help Us
by Christina Anderson

The Moon, The Sun and The Stories We Play
by Dane Figueroa Edidi

Holding
by Zora Howard

SAMUEL FRENCH

It's Complicated © 2024 by Michael Bradford
Thy Will Be Done © 2024 by Dennis A. Allen II
Cliff & Clara & Her Baby © 2024 by Lauren A. Whitehead
Rampjaar © 2024 by James Ijames
Color Theory © 2024 by Eric Micha Holmes
Goddess Help Us © 2024 by Christina Anderson
The Moon, The Sun and The Stories We Play © 2024
by Dane Figueroa Edidi
Holding © 2024 by Zora Howard
All Rights Reserved

THE APOLLO PRESENTS... A NEW HARLEM RENAISSANCE: SHORT PLAYS FROM THE NEW BLACK FEST is fully protected under the copyright laws of the United States of America, the British Commonwealth, including Canada, and all member countries of the Berne Convention for the Protection of Literary and Artistic Works, the Universal Copyright Convention, and/or the World Trade Organization conforming to the Agreement on Trade Related Aspects of Intellectual Property Rights. All rights, including professional and amateur stage productions, recitation, lecturing, public reading, motion picture, radio broadcasting, television, online/digital production, and the rights of translation into foreign languages are strictly reserved.

ISBN 978-0-573-71094-0

www.concordtheatricals.com
www.concordtheatricals.co.uk

FOR PRODUCTION INQUIRIES

UNITED STATES AND CANADA
info@concordtheatricals.com
1-866-979-0447

UNITED KINGDOM AND EUROPE
licensing@concordtheatricals.co.uk
020-7054-7298

Each title is subject to availability from Concord Theatricals Corp., depending upon country of performance. Please be aware that *THE APOLLO PRESENTS... A NEW HARLEM RENAISSANCE: SHORT PLAYS FROM THE NEW BLACK FEST* may not be licensed by Concord Theatricals Corp. in your territory. Professional and amateur producers should contact the nearest Concord Theatricals Corp. office or licensing partner to verify availability.

CAUTION: Professional and amateur producers are hereby warned that *THE APOLLO PRESENTS... A NEW HARLEM RENAISSANCE: SHORT PLAYS FROM THE NEW BLACK FEST* is subject to a licensing fee.

The purchase, renting, lending or use of this book does not constitute a license to perform this title(s), which license must be obtained from Concord Theatricals Corp. prior to any performance. Performance of this title(s) without a license is a violation of federal law and may subject the producer and/or presenter of such performances to civil penalties. Both amateurs and professionals considering a production are strongly advised to apply to the appropriate agent before starting rehearsals, advertising, or booking a theatre. A licensing fee must be paid whether the title(s) is presented for charity or gain and whether or not admission is charged. Professional/Stock licensing fees are quoted upon application to Concord Theatricals Corp.

This work is published by Samuel French, an imprint of Concord Theatricals Corp.

No one shall make any changes in this title(s) for the purpose of production. No part of this book may be reproduced, stored in a retrieval system, scanned, uploaded, or transmitted in any form, by any means, now known or yet to be invented, including mechanical, electronic, digital, photocopying, recording, videotaping, or otherwise, without the prior written permission of the publisher. No one shall share this title(s), or any part of this title(s), through any social media or file hosting websites.

For all inquiries regarding motion picture, television, online/digital and other media rights, please contact Concord Theatricals Corp.

MUSIC AND THIRD-PARTY MATERIALS USE NOTE

Licensees are solely responsible for obtaining formal written permission from copyright owners to use copyrighted music and/or other copyrighted third-party materials (e.g. artworks, logos) in the performance of this play and are strongly cautioned to do so. If no such permission is obtained by the licensee, then the licensee must use only original music and materials that the licensee owns and controls. Licensees are solely responsible and liable for clearances of all third-party copyrighted materials, including without limitation music, and shall indemnify the copyright owners of the play(s) and their licensing agent, Concord Theatricals Corp., against any costs, expenses, losses and liabilities arising from the use of such copyrighted third-party materials by licensees. For music, please contact the appropriate music licensing authority in your territory for the rights to any incidental music.

IMPORTANT BILLING AND CREDIT REQUIREMENTS

If you have obtained performance rights to this title, please refer to your licensing agreement for important billing and credit requirements.

THE APOLLO PRESENTS... A NEW HARLEM RENAISSANCE: SHORT PLAYS FROM THE NEW BLACK FEST were originally commissioned by Keith Josef Adkins of The New Black Fest by a generous grant funded to the Apollo Theater from the Black Seed Fund. The plays were presented on the Apollo Sound Stage during The New Black Fest at the Apollo Theater (Kelley Girod, Director of New Works; Kamilah Forbes, Executive Producer) in New York City on April 22, 23 and 25, 2022. The production manager was Belynda M'baye.

TABLE OF CONTENTS

Foreword 1
by Keith Josef Adkins

Foreword 3
by Kamilah Forbes

It's Complicated 5
by Michael Bradford

Thy Will Be Done 23
by Dennis A. Allen II

Cliff & Clara & Her Baby 37
by Lauren A. Whitehead

Rampjaar 53
by James Ijames

Color Theory 69
by Eric Micha Holmes

Goddess Help Us 85
by Christina Anderson

The Moon, The Sun and The Stories We Play 109
by Dane Figueroa Edidi

Holding 129
by Zora Howard

FOREWORD BY KEITH JOSEF ADKINS

Over a hundred years ago the artists and thinkers of the Harlem Renaissance were living in a world that was chockful of iconic events that shaped and defined the Black community as well as our American society. From the Great Migration, Marcus Garvey's Back to Africa movement and the sanctions of Jim Crow to women's voting rights, the rise and fall of Prohibition and the Great Depression, the creatives and intellectuals of the Harlem Renaissance did what they were destined to do – placed Black people at the center of that world, and provided us with some of the most profound permeations and depictions of Blackness that are still palpable and remembered today.

The world has changed some since the 1920s and social justice and racial pride still headline our lives, but intersectionality, identity politics and the course-correcting of patriarchy appear to stand at the forefront of our community now. Luckily, there is a new generation of playwrights and thinkers who are courageously and creatively interrogating those ideas and factions and they are taking no prisoners. Whether they are aware that they are continuing a century-old legacy or building on one, these new Black artists are here to ensure no stone within Black life is unturned and to remind us Blackness is forever growing, redefining and expanding its borders.

That's why when the Apollo's Executive Producer Kamilah Forbes tasked me with commissioning playwrights to write short plays on the theme of the new Harlem Renaissance I knew it would be an easy thing to do. I know so many of these writers. Eric Micha Holmes, Christina Anderson, Zora Howard, James Ijames, Dennis Allen II – they are my tribe, my community and my inspiration, and they are always ready to quickly engage with and/or reflect on what's currently happening in the world or in their world, much like the Renaissance artists from one hundred years ago.

Their finished, commissioned short plays were exactly what I expected them to be – bold reimaginings and reminders of the beauty, complexity, vulnerability and changing landscape of what it means to be Black and on this planet right now. Kamilah Forbes, Kelly Girod (the Apollo's Director of New Works) and myself were even more thrilled when we shared all the plays during a weekend of sold out performances at the Apollo and a new generation of audiences felt completely seen and heard by these playwrights.

Society and culture has definitely morphed some since the days of the Harlem Renaissance in the 1920s and, in some ways, it hasn't changed much at all (especially with the fear of WOKE culture and the dismantling of DEI), but the presence of artists whose passions and convictions are driven by the deep desire to bear witness to being Black remains a beacon in the community. Without these artists and their legacies I'm not sure we'd know where we've been, where we are now, and what the future holds for us. They must always be located, encouraged, nurtured, shared and be given the flowers for the incredible part they play in society – loving and honoring Black peoples.

Keith Josef Adkins
Artistic Director
The New Black Fest

FOREWORD BY KAMILAH FORBES

It was 2022. As Executive Producer at the Apollo Theater, I was charged with providing a vision for a season for both audiences and artists alike. A season with the goal of basking in the genius and ingenuity of Black arts, artists and culture. We knew our objective was to formulate our 21st century canon initiative that year – building a new canon of Black works. It was during this time that we at the Apollo Theater dove deeply into the inquiry of how our past and future are inextricably linked through the timelessness of our storytellers and stories. The question of how Harlem Renaissance artists responded to the historic events that shaped their time and how contemporary creatives are dealing with the issues of the present moment remained at the center of our inquiry. Our answer would be found through our partnership with The New Black Fest.

Due to their steadfast commitment to amplifying and supporting new work from bright, poignant voices from Black theater, we commissioned The New Black Fest to do what they have a rich reputation of doing across the country and with Black theater. And what an amazing experience and event! The New Black Fest at Apollo Theater brought some of the brightest playwrights together with two dynamic directors and an outstanding ensemble of actors. As part of our diligence to serve as the leading producer and curator of Black Performing Arts, this commission and festival aligned deeply with our mission to produce innovative and inspiring work.

Each play was brilliantly scribed, precisely performed and directed with heart. Audiences leapt to their feet and the plays left an impression on many. From raw and honest characters to plots confronting the challenges of class, stigma, love and joy, these plays from The New Black Fest are both specific and timeless. While the Apollo stands proudly on our legacy of creating culture and history that has informed generations, we eagerly and adamantly commit ourselves to celebrating and supporting the future. The artists whose work you will read in this anthology, and those on a similar journey of writing the plays that tell the stories of our lives, reflect our commitment. Enjoy, and onward in arts and culture.

Kamilah Forbes
Executive Producer
Apollo Theater

It's Complicated

"The Ways of White Folks,"
Langston Hughes

by Michael Bradford

IT'S COMPLICATED was first presented during The New Black Fest at the Apollo Theater on April 23, 2022. The reading was directed by Cezar Williams, with stage directions read by Denise Manning. The cast was as follows:

MASON... Benton Greene
MAGDALENE..................................... Donna Kennedy

CHARACTERS

MASON – Age 40–50, Mason is an African American History Professor from a college in Connecticut. Erudite and charming all at once.

MAGDALENE – Age 40–50, Magdalene is a Caucasian woman whose ancestors once held slaves on the plantation that is now a research center where she is now the Executive Director. She is sincere and forthright.

SETTING

A large Research Center on an old slave-owning plantation located on the outskirts of Savannah, GA. The actual set is minimal, if anything at all, with a few gardening prop pieces and a leather book bag. Elements of sound to support time of day and location are recommended.

TIME

Present day.

(**MAGDALENE** *is dressed for the summer and the garden, floppy hat and all, carrying a wicker basket with flowers hanging over the side. She has a small hand spade and mimes digging.* **MASON** *enters, satchel over his shoulder.*)

MASON. You work here by chance?

MAGDALENE. Yes and no. It's complicated.

MASON. I worry when it isn't.

MAGDALENE. Is there something I can –

MASON. I was hoping to get into the research library.

MAGDALENE. It's closed. Sunday.

MASON. Thought I might get lucky.

Take advantage of a quiet day.

Feels a little strange.

Huge plantation…when it's empty.

MAGDALENE. It's been a library for some time now.

A research library.

MASON. Right.

MAGDALENE. The University in town has a library, it's open every day, has copies of most of what we keep here.

It's open right now if you need to…

I don't know what time they close but…

We open tomorrow at eight, eight to six, if you'd rather…

MASON. Tomorrow's fine.

MAGDALENE. Research, I take it?

MASON. Yeah.

    (Beat.)

MAGDALENE. Most people can't wait to tell you what it's about.

MASON. It's complicated.

MAGDALENE. I worry when it's not.

One of the best research librarians in the state works here.

She'll be here in the morning.

She likes complicated.

MASON. Nice.

    (Sticks out his hand, she shakes it.)

Mason.

MAGDALENE. Magdalene.

MASON. Nice.

I'm staying in Savannah proper and –

MAGDALENE. You figured that out already, the "proper" business.

MASON. My folks, originally from just outside of Savannah.

Used to come down in the summers.

Been a minute since the last time…some things you don't forget.

MAGDALENE. Like "proper."

MASON. Like "proper."

Listen, maybe you know a healthy spot, get a bite to eat.

Open.

On a Sunday.

MAGDALENE. Are you asking me for a recommendation or are you asking me to dinner?

MASON. Let's say...both.

> (**MASON** *helps her to her feet. They walk up center, miming a lively chat as they go. Up center she takes off her hat and sets [hangs] her hat and basket on the floor [or the coat rack]. They turn and start the next dialogue as they walk back down center. They are in Savannah "proper," standing in front of his hotel.)*

Nice recommendation.

The crêpe was amazing.

Light and full and –

MAGDALENE. You sound surprised.

MASON. A bit.

MAGDALENE. New York City is the only place to get an amazing crêpe?

MASON. I can see now it was probably a mistake to mention the big city up "nawth."

MAGDALENE. Just teasing.

(Both smile.)

MASON. Probably tastes the same.

Like most things, context is everything.

Maybe that's why this is feeling a little awkward, *you* walking *me* back to my hotel.

A little backwards.

In context.

MAGDALENE. I'm sure you're aware the whole chivalry thing was always a bit of a myth.

MASON. I am, but I'm just walking and talking and I have no idea where you need to get to. Or how to get you there.

Let me get you an uber or I can take you –

MAGDALENE. I imagine you're going back.

In the morning.

You could take me then.

(A moment.)

MASON. You're right.

I am.

I can.

MAGDALENE. Listen, if you want to kiss me, I think that would be nice.

MASON. Nice.

Yes, I do think that would be…nice.

(They look at each other for a moment, smile, then face upstage. It is the next morning. They are both buttoning their clothes, finishing getting dressed.)

MAGDALENE. A dinner, a walk, a lovely evening and you still haven't told me one thing about your research.

Most people can't wait to tell you!

MASON. I think we had more interesting things to talk about.

Or not talk about.

'Sides, I appreciate it but I think you're just being…nice.

I'm sure you heard a million, dusty, uninteresting –

MAGDALENE. Well I'm officially interested.

   (Both smile.)

MASON. All right.

I'll do my best not to put you to sleep.

I'm documenting the birth, death and genealogy records of plantations with a population of two hundred or more enslaved peoples.

How this affects historical understanding of the internal slave trade after 1807, when Jefferson, bit of irony, outlawed the external slave trade.

Research question, how does our history since affect contemporary relationship patterns and familial structures in predominately African-American communities today.

How much of that experience do we all carry in our DNA, literally and metaphorically.

See.

A little dusty but I tried to keep it interesting.

MAGDALENE. I think it's quite interesting.

   (A moment.)

I'm sure you know Broadwell was a large plantation, but it never had more than a hundred slaves at any one time.

MASON. *Enslaved* people.

And yes. I do know that.

   (A moment.)

My people, my own family, were...enslaved, on one of the three large plantations in this county.

This is clearly outside the scope of my grant but...

MASON. I just need to know where, which one.

If my family knew which plantation, they never talked about it.

By the time I really wanted to know, everybody was passed.

MAGDALENE. This is your first stop?

In this county?

MASON. My last.

MAGDALENE. So...

MASON. Yeah.

I just need to see it. Their names.

Written down.

MAGDALENE. I see.

And once you find the...records, what next?

MASON. No idea.

Maybe a book.

Maybe... I don't really know.

Cross that bridge when it shows up.

MAGDALENE. Well the records at the library are extensive and detailed.

Sadly.

MASON. *(He looks at her.)* I get the feeling you're not just the groundskeeper.

MAGDALENE. It's complicated.

My family left the main house to me.

MASON. Your family?

You mean the –

MAGDALENE. Broadwell family?

Yes.

Magdalene Broadwell was my maiden name.

MASON. I see...

MAGDALENE. Noah Broadwell bought the property in 1687, five generations later here I am.

I never wanted children, so once I set up the research library,

I left everything to the state.

They asked me to stay on, manage the library.

So for all intent and purpose...

MASON. Right, so...

MAGDALENE. So.

Breakfast?

(A moment.)

MASON. Yeah.

Cool.

Breakfast.

(They retreat to opposite sides of the stage. We are now in Magdalene's office at the plantation/library. **MASON** *"enters.")*

MAGDALENE. You've been busy.

MASON. A bit.

MAGDALENE. I hear you've found the records you were looking for.

MASON. I have.

(A moment.)

MAGDALENE. I've been calling for the past week, more.

MASON. I know.

MAGDALENE. Leaving messages on your phone, your room.

Our research librarian.

MASON. She told me

MAGDALENE. We've only seen each other a couple of times, but something... I *thought* something was happening.

No. I know something was happening.

MASON. You're right.

It was...nice.

Something was happening.

MAGDALENE. I told you my name because...of course I should.

I had no idea –

MASON. Really?

No idea?

MAGDALENE. We saw each other again.

You seemed fine.

MASON. You tell me your name, you have to know something like that, at some point, changes *something*.

MAGDALENE. I thought...

Maybe I should feel like a fool.

But I don't. Not at all.

MASON. You don't?

MAGDALENE. You want me to feel like a fool?

MASON. No, I mean...yes.

This feels like a situation –

MAGDALENE. Like a situation that should be black and white?

Like a situation where I *should* feel like a fool?

MASON. I feel like a fool.

A part of me understands it's not the most rational feeling.

But still, yeah, I suppose I thought you might feel the same.

MAGDALENE. Some days I think I would love for life to be that simple, either this or that.

You're either brilliant or you're an idiot.

It's either love or it's not.

For that to be the kind of world we live in.

Is that the kind of world you live in?

MASON. I'm an historian.

I discover, interpret.

Discover something new…reinterpret.

There is no end.

MAGDALENE. But you've come to the end, certainly of your research.

Crossed a few of those bridges you were looking for.

And now you've come to the question of what's next.

So what's next?

MASON. Next is me going back to the New York and –

MAGDALENE. I see.

I suspect we are one of the oldest clichés.

The daughter of slave owners and the son of enslaved people and we've had the audacity to sleep together.

MASON. That's some of it.

MAGDALENE. Some?

MASON. I'm thinking about the men and women in my family, how this history continues, to this day, to devastate my community in ways we aren't even aware of because it's…history.

And then I'm trying to figure out the Broadwell women.

I'm trying to imagine conversations after dinner, around the fire, in the parlor.

In the bedroom.

How do you even begin to understand, to reconcile –

MAGDALENE. Clearly they brought a very different kind of logic to justify the kind of life they wanted.

It's a degree of compartmentalization I haven't even tried to understand.

MASON. Really?

Because I think that's what we're doing, you and me, right now.

MAGDALENE. Am I just lumped in with the "Broadwell women" now?

Only it's my turn to slip out of the house at midnight?

MASON. No, that's not it.

(A moment.)

August 18, 1865 entry, the first line.

"The Union troops have departed and they have all –"

The people who were enslaved, my peoples, who, the day before, were worked from dawn to dusk, whipped and degraded in more ways than –

MAGDALENE. I know what went on here.

MASON. Those people, *my* people, "they ALL came back!"

I was like, this has got be some hyperbole, some kind'a euphemism?

MAGDALENE. It's a family journal, by definition it is not the most objective –

MASON. That's what I'm saying to myself.

I mean, sometimes the entries were downright poetic!

But there it is, right alongside how many pounds of tobacco picked and sold down to the ounce, "August 18th, 1865, they ALL came back."

No hyperbole. No euphemism.

All of them. Every single man, woman, and child.

On the same day. At the same time.

MAGDALENE. I know the story.

MASON. Of course you do! This is some legendary shit!

What the hell?

They must'a been standing at the edge of the clearing, just waiting.

Nobody was talking about, "Go back? Have you lost your damn mind?"

Nobody said, "Alright I know the whole running North thing is a little worrisome, but we know, literally to the bone, the kind of hell we just came from!"

Nobody simply said, "Hell no?!"

MAGDALENE. I'm sure the situation was complicated.

They only knew what they lived.

Someone was telling them to leave but to go where or –

MASON. Complicated.

MAGDALENE. I'm simply saying there were no easy answers.

MASON. And that is the universe we've been living in since 1619.

To this day, there is not one, single easy answer.

And every day somebody is trying to figure out a million ways to not even ask the question.

MAGDALENE. Are you telling me it's too late?

That we can't come to the answers?

I thought I was answering a question when I created this place, held myself accountable.

I thought –

MASON. Magdalene, it's like we're living some circular shit and we haven't figured out how to straighten out this line of history so we can move forward.

MAGDALENE. Does this history have to say anything... about you. Or me.

Right now, in this moment?

MASON. We both know it does.

We act like there's some kind of threshold, some pluralistic utopia we can get to if we just stop treating each other like shit, walking into church and killing people while they're praying just because they don't look like you!

We're like two fish who don't know they're swimming in water.

MAGDALENE. You make it sound like, we're just treading water in the middle of an ocean.

MASON. Some days, we're not even treading.

MAGDALENE. We can't just be two people?

(A moment.)

MASON. I know.

I can see it in your face.

You spent some money.

Did the right thing, opened the family books, turned the place that held people as chattel into a place to critically challenge that notion, that practice.

All of that is great. It is.

And somehow, meeting you, feeling whatever I was feeling, seeing you feeling it, just being two people feeling something...nice, looking up at you sitting on top of me later that night, I knew everything I know right now...and I thought about *none* of it in that moment.

Maybe I was just...digging the fact you were digging me.

Maybe you were... I don't know.

Trust me, there is so much shit we still got to unpack.

It's complicated.

MAGDALENE. I worry when it's not.

MASON. Yeah.

I guess we should all worry.

A little bit.

MAGDALENE. What's next?

MASON. My flight is at –

MAGDALENE. No.

I mean, what's next?

MASON. Magdalene, if I knew the answer to that, we'd be having a very different conversation.

Take good care of yourself.

End of Play

Thy Will Be Done

A ten-minute play
by Dennis A. Allen II

THY WILL BE DONE was first presented during The New Black Fest at the Apollo Theater on April 23, 2022. The reading was directed by Cezar Williams, with stage directions read by Donna Kennedy. The cast was as follows:

PASTOR PAUL .... Benton Greene
MELODY .... Denise Manning

CHARACTERS

PASTOR PAUL – male, 40s
MELODY – female, late 30s–early 40s

SETTING

New Revelations Baptist Church, Harlem – Pastor Paul's Office

TIME

Present

> (**PASTOR PAUL** *stands facing the audience holding a bible in one hand and a small remote control in the other. He wears a black fitted v-neck t-shirt, jeans, and a wooden cross around his neck. He aims the remote at the audience, presses a button then slips the remote into his pocket.)*

PASTOR PAUL. Peace and blessings New Revelations family...

...

Welcome back to a another... ah... hm... no...

...

New Revelations family it's Wednesday again so that means... argh... no...

...

> (**PASTOR PAUL** *reaches back into his pocket, stops the recording, composes himself, then resumes the recording.)*

Welcome to another Won't He Wednesday, I'm Pastor Paul Cummings and we are so happy you are able to virtually join us from wherever you are for today's word. As the second oldest baptist church in Harlem our roots run deep and have nurtured the community with His love for centuries. Remember New Revelations family this coming Sunday we will be back in our Harlem home, praise God, for the first time since the lockdown and so we encourage you to come join us and celebrate His grace, in person, in the flesh, Amen. This community is so special, our diversity is unmatched and I am looking forward to seeing your faith-filled faces as I preach from our pulpit. Of course we will continue to live stream the Sunday sermon for those of us that prefer to receive His word from the comfort of our homes.

Friends, before we get into today's word for Won't He Wednesdays I want to extend a thank you. As you know we recently lost our Youth Pastor and dear brother in Christ, Pastor Derrick, to Covid-19 complications. The support, prayers and donations that you all have showered on the family and our church is a testament, no, is *the* testament of God's love. Pastor Derrick's memorial can still be viewed on our YouTube page and links to donate to the family can be found there and on the New Rev website.

> (**PASTOR PAUL** *takes a moment to clear the despair from his throat.*)

We tend to look at history and only focus on the bad, the evils, the ills of man that repeat over and over again. During the Spanish flu over six hundred thousand Americans died, due to a combination of the disease, inept leadership and a disregard for human life; a third of the population worldwide was snuffed out and we find ourselves one hundred years later in another pandemic//

> (*A door slams. The assertive clicks of high heel shoes echo towards the Pastor's office.*)

MELODY. (*Offstage.*) PAUL!

Paul where you at!

> (**MELODY** *enters. She wears red high heels, jeans, and an off-the-shoulder short sleeve blouse. Tattoos decorate her arms and back, bracelets litter her wrists; she has blonde hair and long ornate fingernails.*)

You're a real muthafucka, you know that?

PASTOR PAUL. Mel you can't come barging into my office like//

MELODY. Fuckalldat. What is your deal?

PASTOR PAUL. I don't know what you mean. I'm working Melody//

MELODY. A real muthafucka.

PASTOR PAUL. God give me strength.

MELODY. Yeah God n' a brain n' a heart too!

...

...

PASTOR PAUL. Are we having a staring contest?

MELODY. Did you know Derrick had a will?

PASTOR PAUL. You didn't?

MELODY. No Paul, I did not. Did you?

PASTOR PAUL. I always advocate that we get our houses in order before we get called home.

MELODY. Nigga da fuck? Ain't nobody ask your preachin' ass for a metaphor.

PASTOR PAUL. Melody...what is wrong?

MELODY. Derrick left everything to the church.

PASTOR PAUL. What do you mean everything?

MELODY. EV-ERY-THING.

PASTOR PAUL. Okay...that's...

MELODY. Don't act like you ain't know.

PASTOR PAUL. I didn't.

MELODY. I don't believe you.

PASTOR PAUL. I make it a point not to meddle in others' relationships.

MELODY. Nigga all you do is meddle. You've dedicated your life to meddling.

PASTOR PAUL. Mel you are hurt and disappointed right now and I understand//

MELODY. Ain't nobody disappointed. I knew you was on that bullshit. Been peeped it since way back. When we was coming up you always had some hustle, some scam goin'. When you went up top and came home all "born again," you had everyone else fooled, Derrick definitely believed in your ass but ME. Nah. This God shit is just another hustle. No different than the gift cards or the IRS calls. That's why you never caught me here on a Sunday.

PASTOR PAUL. Melody I don't know what you want from me.

MELODY. I want You to be straight up for once in your life. All you care about, all you've ever really cared about is money. You ain't stop being a hustla, your hustle just changed. You out here lettin' white tourists sit in the pews, watchin' "the niggers" praise their god, like we monkeys at the zoo.

PASTOR PAUL. *(Mockingly.)* How you know that if you ain't never here?

MELODY. Fuck you Paul!

PASTOR PAUL. Okay.

MELODY. Why you? Why Derrick always choose you? He was my husband. My high school sweetheart. My life. Mine. Not yours. Not yours.

...

...

PASTOR PAUL. Hey. Mel. Sit down. Please. Please.

...

...

You and I have always had a...contentious relationship//

MELODY. Pssh.

PASTOR PAUL. but our love for Derrick and his love for us allowed you and I to bond in a way that we both would've thought impossible, right?

MELODY. I mean "bond" is a strong word, but yeah you held us down during some rough patches. So?

PASTOR PAUL. So…the love isn't gone just because Derrick is no longer physically here. The love is just as strong if not stronger.

MELODY. Paul I ain't come here for no sermon.

PASTOR PAUL. I'm saying

I have no reason to nor would I lie to you. Did we talk about the importance of having a will? Yes. Even before this pandemic, with everything my siblings and I went through when my mother passed, I encouraged folk to have things in order to avoid the mess.

MELODY. I always loved your mom, she was wild. Always kept it real.

PASTOR PAUL. Yeah, real ignorant.

Five kids, three baby daddies, no power of attorney and her, "What I need a will for, I ain't got nothin'." Left us with;

Do we or don't we pull the plug? Do we bury or cremate? Who gets the dog? How do we divvy up the money she had in the mattress?

We just inherited chaos.

MELODY. She had money stashed in her mattress? Daaamn. Miss Cummings was ol' school for real.

…

…

Why wouldn't he talk to me about his will?

PASTOR PAUL. I don't know.

He treated the youth like they were his own, said the church was like his baby and since you two never...

...

...

Look we haven't really had a chance to talk since Derrick died and that's on me.

MELODY. It's on me too.

(A moment.)

PASTOR PAUL. Sooo, I have to finish recording some content and I have a few meetings throughout the day but, if you email Shirley she'll let you know when best we can have a proper sit down.

MELODY. Email Shirley?

PASTOR PAUL. Yeah, you have her email right?

MELODY. You want me to email your secretary to schedule time to talk. To talk about Derrick? Dis nigga here.

...

How much money we got so far?

PASTOR PAUL. Excuse me?

MELODY. You know the GoFundMe "the church" set up for our family. How much we got?

PASTOR PAUL. I haven't checked it recently. You can go to the page yourself and see.

MELODY. Oh you mean the page I don't actually have access to? The one the "church" controls? There are probably donations in Derrick's name coming straight to New Revelations instead of the GoFundMe too huh?

PASTOR PAUL. Some, yes, yeah, Mel just email Shirley, we can sit down together and I'll//

MELODY. Nah. Derrick put me on game. He talked about you doing shit like making the choir director move songs earlier in the service so these gentrifyin' terrorists get a good show. Yeah he said you put on a good show for whitey. Make them think you one of the good ones. You just sooo progressive. Coon nigga shuckin' and jivin' for your white God. Anything for that white dollar.

PASTOR PAUL. I'm a coon? You grown and still act like you did when you was twelve. Maybe Derrick left everything to the church because he didn't want it spent on some Birkin bag or red bottoms – how many Amazon boxes were stacked outside your door this morning before you came to see me?

MELODY. Hol' up! How bout we open up the books and track every single dolla that comes through these doors then see how high and mighty the great "Pastor Paul" is? Maybe an anonymous call to the Feds, get them to use a fine tooth comb on your ass.

PASTOR PAUL. I have nothing to hide.

MELODY. Give. Me. My. MON-NEY!

PASTOR PAUL. What you want me to write you a check right here? That's not//

MELODY. I don't care if it's cash, credit, cowrie shells or mutha fuckin' Bitcoin, nigga come up off mine!

PASTOR PAUL. I can't right now. Just//

MELODY. What you use to pay for those private planes you all over the world in? That brownstone you got your side piece livin' the good ol' life in.

Uh huh, yeah that fund. Go on and pay me my due outta that. Mister high and mighty you real quiet over there. Like I said, you the same lame lyin' thief you always was. Trash. I don't know what Derrick saw in you.

PASTOR PAUL. When I took over the church fifteen years ago there were three hundred members; now we have over ten thousand. We have ministries worldwide because of me and my commitment to our community//

MELODY. GOOD FOR YOU...

PASTOR PAUL. When have you ever contributed to anything? I'm a coon? I'm trash? I know hurt people, hurt people but you comin' at me like...

MELODY. Yeah. Yeah.

PASTOR PAUL. You not the only one grieving Derrick. Actually, you are, 'cause I don't have time to grieve and all I do is grieve. Do you know where I go in those private planes? You know how many funerals and memorials I've done this year alone? Not just due to Covid but the damn shootings, stabbings, police shootings, cancer, diabetes, I have to preside over weddings, virtual meetings, hold politicians accountable, keep the staff paid, my family fed, the homeless fed and and and... AND how Derrick get Covid? Huh Melody?

MELODY. Don't do that.

PASTOR PAUL. How many times did Derrick beg you to wear a mask? Not to fly to Atlanta so you can party with your peeps? Why did he leave everything to the church? Because the only responsible relationship he was in – was with God.

...

...

Melody I'm sorry. That was too//

MELODY. You know what's crazy? I was good with livin' with the guilt that I was the reason Derrick got sick. Livin' with that truth everyday for the rest of my life feels just. I deserve to live a tormented life. But knowing that he valued an institution more than me...

he loved... more than me... Before I leave this earth I'm going to expose you for the fraud you are.

> (**MELODY** *storms out.* **PASTOR PAUL** *takes a moment. Reaches in his pocket, takes out the remote and presses the button. Takes another moment then presses the button again.*)

PASTOR PAUL. *(Waves of emotion.)* During the Spanish flu over six hundred thousand Americans died, a third of the population worldwide snuffed out and we find ourselves one hundred years later in another pandemic. Grief is a powerful force and if we're not careful, the pain grief causes can have us doubting everything. Who we are, who we love, the point of existence... is there a God?

Romans chapter twelve verse two tells us, "And be not conformed to this world: but be transformed by the renewing of your mind, that you may prove what is that good, and acceptable, and perfect, will of God." Disease. Pain. Grief. Death. They make it hard not to conform to this world.

Do you know what else happened one hundred years ago just after the Spanish flu ravaged the world? This thing we now know as the Harlem Renaissance. Coming out of a pandemic and towards the Great Depression, artists, Black artists created some of the most influential, inspiring work the world had ever seen. Right here in Harlem.

"And be not conformed to this world: but be transformed by the renewing of your mind." These young brothers and sisters renewed their minds and transformed not only themselves but the world. That was God's will. Good, acceptable and perfect will.

You may feel like you've conformed to the patterns of this world; given in to grief, paralyzed by pain, frozen in fear but that's okay. No one is perfect. No man is perfect. To be transformed you have to renew your mind and know that the mind is weak but your spirit is strong, faith is strong, God's love is strong. We can all be renewed. That is His promise. His good, pleasing and perfect will.

Won't he do it?

Come on and join us on Sunday and see if we can get our minds, our spirits, our hearts renewed. Amen.

(He takes out the remote and presses the button.)

End of Play

Cliff & Clara & Her Baby

A ten-minute play
by Lauren A. Whitehead

CLIFF & CLARA & HER BABY was first presented during The New Black Fest at the Apollo Theater on April 23, 2022. The reading was directed by Cezar Williams, with stage directions read by Benton Greene. The cast was as follows:

CLARA...Denise Manning
CLIFF..Ethan Dubin

CHARACTERS

CLARA – Black. Young-ish. Eight months pregnant.
CLIFF – White. The same age-ish as Clara.

SETTING

Brooklyn.

TIME

The high heat of summer.

(Lights up on **CLIFF** *and* **CLARA** *sitting on a couch in an apartment that is incredibly neat and obviously cobbled together from garage sales and thrift stores. Despite its order, there is a large, disheveled corner crowded with all manner of baby projects in progress, each of them in various states of completion.)*

*(***CLARA** *is working as hard as she can to be as quiet as she can while retrieving and eating chips from a family-sized bag. She is black. Young-ish. Eight months pregnant, wearing overalls with a sports bra. It is the high heat of summer. Brooklyn. Fireworks and police sirens and helicopters and loud-talkin'-ass neighbors are just kind of always happening in the background.)*

*(***CLIFF** *is sitting on the floor, midway through building some elaborate nursery item. He is white. The same age-ish as* **CLARA**. *And while his hands are absolutely full, he's sitting stiffly, still and listening intently.)*

(A scurry is happening somewhere in the apartment that is inaudible to everyone except **CLARA**.*)*

CLARA. See there! There! Did you hear it?

(She struggles to get up. Gives up.)

Did you hear it?! Over there!

*(***CLIFF** *doesn't move.)*

CLIFF. I didn't hear it.

CLARA. Shhh...

CLIFF. Stop eating chips for a second so I can hear.

CLARA. I can't stop eating chips, love. The chips need me.

CLIFF. Well, I'm not gonna be able to hear anything over the bag of –

CLARA. Shh! There it is again! By the stove.

> *(They listen as she still tries to get a chip. He looks at her lovingly and also frustratedly.)*

CLIFF. For real?

CLARA. We have a mouse.

> *(She rubs crumbs off the top of her belly and on to the floor. She closes the bag of chips and puts them on the other side of the couch.* **CLIFF** *gets up to get a hand vacuum.)*

CLIFF. Yes. I know. I'm taking care of it.

CLARA. I'm not bringing my baby into a house with a mouse.

CLIFF. *(Sing songy alongside her.)* You're not bringing our baby into a house with a mouse... Yes, love. I know.

CLARA. I'm not.

CLIFF. I know. *(Beat.)* You're bringing our baby into a house *infested* with mice.

CLARA. STOP IT!

> *(**CLARA** reaches for the chips and begins eating them again.)*

CLIFF. Can you just trust me?

CLARA. Fine.

CLIFF. Good. Now let me ask you this...

CLARA. What?

CLIFF. Would you bring our baby into a boat with a coat?

(A holding back of laughter kind of beat on his part.)

Would you bring our baby into a park after dark?

CLARA. It's really unattractive.

CLIFF. Last one, last one: would you bring our baby into a –

CLARA. Shh! See, there it is again! Did you hear it?

(A very loud firecracker whistles and pops very close to the window.)

CLIFF. Can't hear shit actually. Annnnd yep, like clockwork, here come the helicopters.

*(Helicopters flying overhead and meanwhile **CLARA** is drinking so much water.)*

CLARA. It'll pass.

CLIFF. I don't think it will but I *do* think that it's a conspiracy.

CLARA. A conspiracy to do what?

CLIFF. Torture us. Enrage us. Exhaust us so we'll stop marching and protesting.

CLARA. I can't talk about the protests boo... I just can't engage that right now. Me and Baby just need – we just need –

*(She's struggling again to get herself up. **CLIFF** helps her and once on her feet, she waddles to the fridge, opens both of the doors and maneuvers her belly into the fridge and her face and shoulders into the freezer. It's clear she's done this before.)*

Between the heat and the hormone dreams, my blood pressure is just...

CLIFF. Yea, but that's my point. The whole point is to make us feel like powerless, paranoid wrecks until we're so anxious we give up and just accept that we can't do shit about the perpetual trauma of living in a police state.

(Beat.)

CLARA. *(From inside the freezer.)* I'm not sure it's about you so much, boo, but...

CLIFF. What?

CLARA. Nothing. Let's go over the plans again, yea?

CLIFF. I'm not hearing you from inside the –

CLARA. *(Louder now.)* LET'S GO OVER THE PLANS AGAIN.

CLIFF. Clara, no. I don't want – we got it, okay?

CLARA. Can you just –

CLIFF. It's just not really fun to imagine all the worst case scenarios, you know?

(She comes out of the freezer eating ice cream out of a half gallon with a spoon.)

CLARA. I'm a black woman in America, my love, of course I know.

CLIFF. Do you keep a spoon in the freezer?

CLARA. I decided to cut out the middleman...

CLIFF. The middleman being... The walk to the silverware drawer?

CLARA. Exactly. I just keep it in the carton now. It's much, much easier.

CLIFF. Can't tell if I'm impressed or disgusted.

CLARA. It can be both, babe. It's both. Free your mind, alright. *(Beat.)* Alright, should we start?

CLIFF. If we have to.

CLARA. Yes. Let's run through the scenario where Baby has already been delivered and now I'm experiencing pain that everybody thinks is normal even though I feel like it's not...

(He is clearly dreading this practice.)

CLIFF. Okay. Is it normal or is it not?

CLARA. Doesn't matter cause I feel like it's not.

CLIFF. Yea, but it *does* matter because if it's only a feeling then we talked about how you would prefer it if I encouraged you to do some self-reflecting before we went into crisis prevention.

CLARA. Okay, let's not get into all that part right now.

CLIFF. Well, I don't know which protocol to implement if the scenario isn't clear.

CLARA. Yes, dear, but that's the reality of the situation. The scenario will never be clear. Like it's all going to be fuzzy and unpredictable.

CLIFF. Or maybe it'll be just fine.

CLARA. Maybe it'll be better if we were prepared.

CLIFF. Okay, then, for the sake of practice, which protocol –

CLARA. For the sake of practice, let's say I've self-reflected but I still feel like it's not normal, okay? Jesus. Fuck.

(A single firecracker whistles and pops.)

CLIFF. Maybe we should practice at another time.

CLARA. Maybe you should practice trusting me when I talk about my feelings.

CLIFF. To be clear, we are talking about your made up feelings in a made up scenario right now, right? Yes.

CLARA. Whatever, Cliff. Can we just... let's just say that I'm experiencing pain that is not normal and the nurse just got finished telling me that it will subside and she's getting ready to leave. What do you say?

CLIFF. I say, "ma'am" – or sir – "my wife is in pain, could you please check her symptoms again?"

CLARA. She reassures you that she's checked the charts, she still tries to walk out and you say...

CLIFF. I say, "sir, I insist that you check her numbers again. I've read reports about postpartum pain and –"

(A buzzer rings.)

Oh, thank god.

(He runs to the door. It's a man with a package.)

Did you order something?

CLARA. Oh boo, I've ordered so many things.

CLIFF. Right.

CLARA. Open it! Maybe it's a gift. I hope it's the bottle box. Or the pacifiers... I can't believe that any day now I'm gonna have a squishy little bugaboo who's gonna be sucking on a wittle pacifier like a perfectly perfect little –

*(**CLARA**'s language devolves into a gibberish of baby talk as she addresses her belly directly. Meanwhile **CLIFF** is opening the package. It contains various things.)*

CLIFF. Onesies. More onesies. Long onesies. Dress onesies... Don't know what *this* is and...mousetraps.

CLARA. Oh! Right.

CLIFF. You ordered mousetraps?

CLARA. Yea, I just thought –

CLIFF. Of course you ordered mousetraps.

CLARA. I just figured if I was already ordering that I would also –

CLIFF. You just figured you would do it for me because you didn't think I was on top of –

CLARA. No, I just thought that because I was already ordering a bunch of other stuff that I would –

CLIFF. Yea, but *why* when I told you I was gonna take care of it?

CLARA. I know. And you still can. I was only thinking about cutting out the middleman...

CLIFF. And in this case the middleman is *me*?

CLARA. No, that's not what I meant –

CLIFF. You can't trust me to kill a mouse /

CLARA. / It's not about trust, okay –

CLIFF. – but you wanna trust me to make sure the doctors don't kill you.

CLARA. You're being a little dramatic now.

CLIFF. No. No. It is about trust. You don't think I have what it takes to handle messy shit.

CLARA. What are you talking about?

(Fireworks. Helicopters. Neighbors. Etc. It's hard to tell whether the couple is getting louder because of the environment or because of the circumstances.)

CLIFF. Oh come on, Clara. For months now you've been asking me for my input on all this stuff but then you turn around and do everything your own way anyway.

CLARA. Is this about painting the crib because I told you we can keep the plain pine if you're really invested in that.

CLIFF. No, it's not about painting the crib. You've always done this. For years.

CLARA. Years?

CLIFF. Years.

CLARA. What exactly have I done for years?

CLIFF. You know what... Never mind. It's not worth it.

CLARA. I knew this couldn't be about mousetraps because that's just not a big deal.

CLIFF. But it is a big deal. It is. Crib color is a big deal, these baby wearing things are a big deal, these organic crib sheets and organic blankies – as if our baby was going to EAT the bedding – all of it is a big deal TO YOU and so I've let you have those things. I've let you manage and decide and this thing, this one thing was mine. So maybe mousetraps don't feel like a big deal to you but I've been telling you that I would take care of it and it's clear you don't –

CLARA. Yea, you've been telling me that but you still haven't done it.

(Silence.)

You haven't taken care of it. And here I am *so* pregnant I can barely bend over or breathe and the baby could come literally any second now and there's still so much to do and I can't be that helpful and the last thing I want is to have to be worried about whether or not our apartment will be full of vermin when I bring my baby home from –

CLIFF. Our baby.

CLARA. What?

CLIFF. *Our* baby.

CLARA. Well obviously *our* baby, Cliff.

CLIFF. Yea, but you always say, "my baby."

CLARA. You wanna have a conversation about semantics when I'm telling you that I'm worried about our apartment being full of mice?

CLIFF. Yea, but that's the thing. You don't have to worry because I said I would take care of it. If I say, I'll handle it, you should take that worry off of your plate because it's being handled.

CLARA. I guess.

CLIFF. You guess?

CLARA. I'm just –

CLIFF. What? Say it.

CLARA. No, forget it.

CLIFF. Say it!

CLARA. Well, fucking when, Cliff? When?

CLIFF. When what?

CLARA. When, exactly, were you going to handle it? Because I've been talking about the mouse for weeks now. WEEKS! I've been pregnant for months. In hip and back and chest pain for months and saying to you every day that between the helicopters and firecrackers and nosy ass Theresa next door telling me that our hospital of choice is an absolute death trap for pregnant black women, every day I've been telling you that I can't sleep because of my belly and also because all night long I hear the scurrying fucking mouse behind the walls so like... I just got tired of waiting and I decided to order the mousetraps on my own. I just decided to take care of it.

CLIFF. So all this time that I've been building cribs and bassinets and car seats and bolting bookshelves into the walls while you've been making me go through these traumatic scenarios over and over again, imagining your death, imagining bringing *our* baby home without you, all this time you've been making me practice my little speeches – *doctor, my wife is still in pain and we need you to do something. Sir, if she says she feels funny, I would like for you to check again. No, check again. Check again check again check again* like I wouldn't have the wherewithal to handle it if something goes wrong at the hospital. All this time I've been doing all that and somewhere in your head you've got your own separate plan to take care of it yourself?

CLARA. And so what if I do, Cliff? You know, not everything is about your fragile manhood, okay?

CLIFF. Wow.

CLARA. Not everything is about you! It's about the facts. And the fact is I could die in there, okay? It's a real thing. I could die on that table. I could die on the sidewalk on the way to that table. I could die in a library or in a church or in my car driving to the grocery store and I don't want to die. All I want to do is hold my –

CLIFF. Our!

CLARA. *This* baby I've been building in *my* body for all this time without some rabies-ridden rodent in my kitchen.

CLIFF. Yea, but you won't let me help you!

> *(A mouse has appeared, eating the crumb of a potato chip by the oven in the kitchen. The firecrackers, which have been increasingly loud and frequent over the previous moment have reached a peak and **CLIFF** can't take it. He spots the mouse in the corner of his eye, grabs the disassembled leg of a high chair from the large pile of baby stuff in the corner and runs screaming at it like a warrior.)*

CLIFF. AHHHHHHHHHH!

CLARA. What the –

> *(The mouse scurries under the oven and **CLIFF** commences beating on the oven with the leg of the chair. It makes a loud metallic clang punctuating his next line.)*

CLIFF. MY WIFE WILL NOT BRING HER BABY INTO A HOUSE WITH A MOUSE!

> *(**CLIFF** has exhausted himself. He slumps onto the floor in front of the oven. Sweating. Hot. Sad. Frustrated. **CLARA** wants to laugh but doesn't.)*

CLARA. Did you get him?

CLIFF. Don't make fun of me, love.

CLARA. I'm sorry.

CLIFF. I'm trying my best.

CLARA. I know.

> *(**CLARA** comes over to sit next to him. It takes a long time for her to get down.)*

CLIFF. I'm scared.

CLARA. Me too, boo. But I'm *more* scared.

CLIFF. I know in my head that that has to be true but in my heart, I still feel like – okay, yea, she's scared and she has a *right* to be, a whole series of generations of reasons to be legitimately afraid. But I'm also scared and I don't feel like… it just feels like I'm not allowed to – like I don't deserve to be as scared as I am. I'm so tired. And so behind. AND SO ANNOYED WITH THESE FUCKING HELICOPTERS! So I just wanted to get the mouse. I really, really wanted to get him.

(**CLARA** *struggles to get up off the floor. It takes a long, long time. She retrieves the ice cream from the freezer, slides back down the fridge and hands it to* **CLIFF**.)

CLIFF. You stood all the way up, by yourself, just for me?

CLARA. I did.

CLIFF. Because you love me?

CLARA. I do.

(*A beat, while he eats some ice cream.*)

CLIFF. It really is genius to just keep the spoon...

CLARA. Right there in the carton.

CLIFF. Best to be prepared.

CLARA. I told you.

(*Lights out.*)

Rampjaar

by James Ijames

RAMPJAAR was first presented during The New Black Fest at the Apollo Theater on April 23, 2022. The reading was directed by Goldie Patrick, with stage directions read by Lynnette Freeman. The cast was as follows:

GENE . . . . Russell G. Jones
VANCE . . . . Ashley Monet

CHARACTERS

GENE – A security guard at the museum.
VANCE – A visitor, an art student.

SETTING

An art museum. A big one. Like the Met.

TIME

I'm trying to do real time…but…we'll see.

AUTHOR'S NOTE

Rampjaar is a dutch word that loosely translates to "disaster year."

(*An art museum. A big one. Like the Met. The din of a crowd dwindling. Over the speaker we hear an announcement that the museum is closing in ten minutes.*)

(*On the wall is a portrait. Dutch Renaissance. Dark, lovely, expensive. It is hanging on the fourth wall.*)

(*In front of the painting is a bench. A museum bench. Simple. Bright pine. A rich person's name etched on a little slip of brass.*)

(*Sitting on the bench, in front of the painting, is **VANCE**. She studies it. She has been sitting in front of the painting for hours. I would say since right after the museum opened.*)

(**GENE** *is watching from the side. He has been watching **VANCE** at least since lunch.*)

GENE. You know we bout to close right?

VANCE. Hmm? What?

GENE. How long you been here?

VANCE. I think I got here around nine.

GENE. Okay, art lover! You just spent the whole day? That's nice, that's nice.

VANCE. Yes.

GENE. Aw! I love that... the appreciation you're showing here. I like to see people appreciate the art.

VANCE. Do you have a favorite?

GENE. This one actually. Something about it. I feel like I've looked at it so long, it's a part of me. It's mine.

VANCE. It is yours.

GENE. Huh. Right! I suppose it is now. On like a spiritual level. Deep sis.

VANCE. Few years ago I was in the beauty salon getting my hair done and there was this TV show where this woman was holding a piece of china.

GENE. Okay.

VANCE. The woman and the china were almost the same color. She called the china, Wedgwood.

GENE. If you're looking for household pieces, that's two floors up. I think there's some Wedgwood in there. If you hurry I think you could probably see them.

VANCE. I couldn't care less what Wedgwood was but suddenly I felt like it was important. The whole image was telling me to pay attention. I was supposed to know what it meant. Why else would this nice porcelain white lady be telling me that the tea cup she was holding was Wedgwood. They were all neoclassical in style. I didn't know what neoclassical was, having not yet gone to graduate school to study art history.

GENE. OHHHHH! You're a student!

VANCE. Yes.

GENE. Here we go. I was getting so confused. But now I understand. I see the art students in here all the time. You don't really give me that energy.

VANCE. What energy is that?

GENE. Just sort of...emo.

VANCE. That's...really accurate.

GENE. I'm an observer. But I interrupted you. Neoclassical?

VANCE. Yeah. When I learned the term in school, I understood it... It was meant for me to understand it. That's no mistake. It's intentional.

GENE. What?

VANCE. The white lady with the white cup in a style that we're supposed to believe is the origin of goodness, of civilization, of beauty, of reason, of intellect. But in real life...it's a bunch of dishes. Its goodness requires my acquiescence. My belief in a lie.

> (**GENE** *stares at* **VANCE.** *She is still studying the painting. An announcement over the speaker system says something about how much time visitors have in the museum.*)

GENE. Uh huh. Well. You're welcome to stay a bit longer but...we're closing soon.

VANCE. I'm going to take this painting with me.

GENE. What you mean?

VANCE. Yeah...that's what I'm going to do.

GENE. I... I don't think you can.

VANCE. Sure I can. Someone brought it in here.

> (**GENE** *is confused. Wait a minute...*)

GENE. Oop! Is this a prank show. Ha! I always thought someone should prank one of us. It makes sense. Where's the camera?

VANCE. No. No candid camera. No pranking. This ain't a joke. I'm gonna take it.

GENE. Uh... Miss... I'm gonna –

VANCE. – It belongs to me.

GENE. I believe it belongs to the museum.

VANCE. I could change your mind.

GENE. Miss...

VANCE. She is rather ordinary looking isn't she?

GENE. Who?

VANCE. The woman in the painting. That's Dina Vinke. Her husband was a Dutch businessman who lost everything in the tulip crash and then made his fortune in the trade of African people. He had this painting done to commemorate the birth of their first child.

GENE. Oh. Interesting.

VANCE. It is. The ship in the background there. Do you see it?

GENE. Yes.

VANCE. It's called De Weduwe which translates to The Widow. On the ship's final voyage from Ghana to the Dutch colonies in the Caribbean an illness ripped through the ship and the captain, Dina's husband. He made the executive decision to throw all of the sick captives overboard in order to recoup the insurance on the cargo... the cargo... the people...

GENE. That really happened?

VANCE. It did. So when the ship finally made it to the port in New Amsterdam, a woman disembarked. I don't know what her name was but they called her Lucky. Cause she had survived the ordeal. She gave birth to Hank who begot Winnie and Grace. Grace was sold to a planter in Georgia who took a fancy to lighting the skirt tails of the servant girls on fire to watch them. Her daughter's name was Ishtar and she had a slew of boys. The youngest being Caleb who had nothing but girls much to the chagrin of the planter. His eldest daughter Patsy bore many children. Somebody say she was pregnant the majority of her life. Tonk was her last son and was sold off to a planter who was also a senator in the congress of the new nation that he lived in called the United States... It goes on from there... Peg and Willy and Marcellus and Caesar, Placidly and Harmony and Grace. But Herbert Jr. knew nothing of slavery and his daughter Grace gave birth to an intrepid young woman she named Helen who worked her way through school and married a man who worked as hard as she did. They had a daughter who they encouraged to follow her dreams. And here. I. Is.

GENE. You?

VANCE. Me.

GENE. How do you know all of that?

VANCE. I'm really good at research.

GENE. Damn.

(**GENE** *looks at the woman in the painting.*)

What happened to her?

VANCE. Not sure. I imagine she and her husband went on being rich and selling people. Do you think she knew?

GENE. Who?

VANCE. Dina? What was gonna happen? What was possible? The cost of ease...

(**GENE** *considers this.*)

GENE. Yes.

VANCE. Really?

GENE. Yes. How could she not. She...

VANCE. Just didn't care.

(*The museum is mostly empty by now.*)

GENE. I don't think I can let you take the painting.

VANCE. Sure you can. You just turn a blind eye.

GENE. Look, I think it's best if you just be on your way and we can act like this didn't happen.

VANCE. How many Black people does this painting cost?

GENE. How many –

VANCE. – How many Black men, women and children does that painting cost? That one right there. How many indigenous people do you imagine? Put a number to it? Six? Eighteen? Forty-five? How many?

GENE. I don't know.

VANCE. Of course you don't. I don't either it is properly innumerable. You don't know, or rather you can't possibly know how many because you can't, how could you conceive of using people as currency, or keeping them as property...

GENE. I can't.

VANCE. But you still feel it in your bones. That's the trick of all of this. You are distracted into thinking everything is work while a lie tears out your insides. I'm Vance by the way.

GENE. I would normally say nice to meet you Vance.

VANCE. But this isn't a normal interaction.

GENE. It is not.

VANCE. Come sit with me.

GENE. Hmmm?

VANCE. Oh Gene! Bruh! The day's almost over... just sit.

GENE. How you know my name?

VANCE. Name tag.

GENE. Hmph.

VANCE. Come on. Sit.

(**GENE** *walks over and sits beside* **VANCE**. *He is uneasy but weirdly drawn in. What iiiiis her deal?*)

GENE. What kind of art do you study?

VANCE. These guys. The Dutch Masters.

GENE. Like the cheap cigars they make blunts with?

VANCE. WOW! Well...yeah.

GENE. You study cheap cigars?

VANCE. No... I... there were these Dutch painters. Rembrandt, Vermeer, Bray. I study them.

GENE. Hmm?

VANCE. Don't approve?

GENE. I mean. Don't you want to look at some people that look like you.

VANCE. Yeah. And I do. But... I don't know... the painting just sort of found me.

GENE. No offense at all but... I mean...

VANCE. I thought...maybe they could unlock something for me?

GENE. What?

VANCE. How to get back what I lost?

GENE. What you mean?

VANCE. All of these cost something.

GENE. They say they priceless but... hmmph.

VANCE. No such thing... it's us. You and me. We are the price of these paintings. The price is that we will look at them and aspire to what we see.

GENE. You wanna look like them?

VANCE. No.

GENE. Then what you talking about?

VANCE. We have to start taking what belongs to us. These buildings full of art by dead men who got paid with the money made from our ancestors' theft, toil, murder, and dehumanization.

GENE. That painting right there?

VANCE. This one in particular.

GENE. Huh.

VANCE. I first saw it on a little postcard in the gift shop... I bought the postcard and put it up on my wall above my desk. Just the motivation I needed to finish my dissertation. Every day I looked at it. Something about it cried out for correction. Kept me up at night. I would lie awake at night and think about it. One day I thought I would come see it in person. I would sit with it. See if it would let me rest. I tarried up with that painting night and day. I couldn't figure out what was happening initially. Was I self-loathing? Was I idealizing this image because it was different from me. Because of its whiteness. And then about two months ago I was sitting here watching the painting. Watching people stopped and stared. And it seemed blood started to flow from the painting.

GENE. Blood.

VANCE. Yeah.

GENE. Whose blood?

VANCE. Hundreds, thousands of people ground into bloody pulp to make this work of art possible to make this country possible, this city, this museum. The blood poured from every crack, every corner... it spilled all over the floor, all over me... it ran down the stairs into the street and pooled up in front of the building. I followed it. Tried to stop it... to staunch the bleeding. But it kept coming. And the screams.

GENE. People were frightened? By the blood?

VANCE. No… the blood was screaming. It was so loud. Like cicadas bursting from beneath the ground in defiant wrathful resurrection. Once you hear it…you can't un-hear it. Can you hear it?

GENE. No.

VANCE. Look at the painting.

GENE. I'm looking.

VANCE. Listen.

GENE. I don't –

> *(A wail is heard and then quickly extinguished.* **GENE** *shudders.)*

VANCE. There.

GENE. What was that?

VANCE. Keep listening.

> *(Another wail. More persistent. Painful and completely in possession of its humanity.* **GENE** *is visibly rattled… The museum is empty. Desolate.* **GENE** *tries to speak over the wails.)*

GENE. How do you hear yourself think?

VANCE. I don't.

GENE. Does it ever shut off?

VANCE. Not once you hear it. Not once you see what's really inside of these things.

GENE. What is it?

VANCE. A lie.

GENE. A what?

VANCE. A lie!

GENE. What is the lie...

VANCE. That we belong, below, with a boot on our neck. That we are ugly. Brutish. Evil. Sinful.

GENE. I don't believe that!

VANCE. You don't have to... A fish doesn't have to believe there is water to swim through it.

GENE. What do we do?

VANCE. Tell the truth.

GENE. Make it stop!

VANCE. Tell the truth.

GENE. Please! Just stop it. STOP!

VANCE. You gotta speak your truth!

GENE. I hate guarding this place. I hate that everything within these walls is valued more than my life. I hate that nothing in here looks like me. I hate that I'm invisible to these patrons. I hate this place!

(The sound is snuffed out. Like a gasp.)

*(**GENE** stands looking at the painting. He looks at **VANCE** then at the painting. He sits beside **VANCE**. Quite changed.)*

Do they all sound like that?

VANCE. Yeah. The Rembrandts, the Monets, the Manets and the Picassos. Don't get me started on the Picassos. She's noisy.

GENE. It wasn't new.

VANCE. What?

GENE. The sound? Was just louder.

VANCE. I suppose that is what it feels like.

GENE. What do you do with a lie that is so big you can't turn it around to truth?

VANCE. You set it on fire.

GENE. You have a real destructive streak.

VANCE. Perhaps.

GENE. You walking around with that much screaming in your head?

VANCE. You are too.

GENE. Not like that.

VANCE. You are… you just figured out a way to make it sound like music.

GENE. Hmm.

VANCE. I best be on my way.

GENE. Are you going to…

VANCE. Yes.

GENE. Wait, though…

VANCE. What?

GENE. What…what you gonna do with it? Like…you can't sell it… you gonna walk up in an auction talking bout "I got Rembrandts and Brays." You can't do nothing with… what you gonna do…

VANCE. Whatever the hell I want. Because, what I do with things that belong to me? I do. As. I. Please.

> (**VANCE** *walks over to the painting and reaches to pluck it off the wall.*)
>
> (*Blackout.*)
>
> (*An alarm goes off.*)

(The fluorescent lights flicker back on.)

*(**GENE** stands and looks at where the painting once was.)*

(He listens and listens and listens.)

GENE. Well... Done with the screaming blood I see. Let me go on and treat myself to a piece or two. That'll be hot. A little Rembrandt in my bathroom.

(He exits.)

Color Theory

by Eric Micha Holmes

COLOR THEORY was first presented during The New Black Fest at the Apollo Theater on April 22, 2022. The reading was directed by Cezar Williams, with stage directions read by Portia. The cast was as follows:

MAN... Benton Greene
WOMAN... Denise Manning

CHARACTERS

MAN & WOMAN – Black, late 30s, upwardly-mobile transplants to Harlem.

SETTING

Blank stage. Two stools.

TIME

Post-pandemic Harlem.

AUTHOR'S NOTES

Act breaks are transitional spaces the director is invited to explore with staging, music, design, blocking, and/or emotional adjustments.

ACT ONE

(**MAN** *and* **WOMAN**.)

(*They talk to us.*)

MAN. I walked in on them. They were on my bed. *Our* bed. It was an engagement gift to ourselves, so there was something ironic...*tragic*. Tragic about seeing them laying on our bed. Splayed out...serene. Almost inviting. Like they were daring me to find them. And that's when I did it. I had to. There was no way I would not. So I did.

(*Beat.*)

I put on my wife's panties.

WOMAN. He's married. And I have a four-year-old daughter in a two bedroom in the one-fifties. But he has his own business so we always had a place to go.

MAN. Pink. Pale but not rosé. Vivid but not fuchsia. Lacey but modern. Think "pink" and that's the color they were...*perfect*.

WOMAN. We met at work. This was before the pandemic. We didn't meet *at* work, we met *while* we were working because I'm in Communications for this arty non-profit you never heard of. And he was doing some drywall in the office.

MAN. The house was a mess. Karen just got back from a trip so her clothes were everywhere and... yes, okay, my wife's name is Karen. And, yes, Karen is white. I'm sorry. It's not her fault. We cannot choose who we fall in love with; and we sure as shit can't choose their name.

WOMAN. We started... I won't say "dating" but we started hooking up. Every other weekend or so. More when the pandemic hit.

MAN. So I'm standing in front of a mirror wearing Karen's pink panties. And this is not the part of the story where I, like, *discovered* I'm a woman or whatever. If I learned anything it's that I could lose a couple pounds. I'd put on a good COVID-20. The panty line, like, zagged across my junk... my gut folded over the sides and the hair... agh...so much hair...

WOMAN. It wasn't great, the, uh...sex. I mean, it was *fine*. Which is what I wanted. I wanted something soft... familiar. Fine. I'm working from home, schools were canceled, I'm a single mother, and my daughter is...not fine.

MAN. My wife and me, we stopped... I mean, you know... since the pandemic? And it's not because we didn't want to. It's because we just, like, *forgot* to – so nature took our bodies back. "This," I thought when I looked in the mirror, "*This* is what a thirty-seven-year-old man's body looks like." Without gyms. Without showers and a tight fade and giving a shit. *Decolonized*. This is my big, fat, hairy, decolonized, Blackity-Black-Black body.

(Beat.)

Wearing panties.

(Beat.)

To be honest? I never felt more masculine.

WOMAN. He was guilty and I liked that. I liked that he was unavailable. I wanted something I could give up.

MAN. I took the panties off and I laid 'em back on the bed. I cannot stress enough how...*uneventful* this was. Probably? I'd have never remembered putting them on. If not for what happened next:

WOMAN. I'm not a casual person. Unhealthy attachment is my jam. But this was the summer of 2020 when we all did things out of character. The pressure. Work alone was enough to… look, I'm not even gonna get into work because it's boring since my boss is… I mean, he's a nice guy. White. Very *nice* and very white and he started doing this thing, in the weeks after George Floyd and the marches and all that, he kept going out of his way to, like, *compliment* me at staff meetings. Thanking me, over and over again for just, like, doing my job. He'd even give me credit for things I didn't do. It was extra. My girlfriends were like *(Snapping.)* "Get it, girl! Reparations." But… I don't know…I guess I just don't like that kind of attention. So…

   (Pause.)

…it was around that time I slept with a married man.

MAN. Later that morning, Karen finds me in the hallway and says, casually, almost like an afterthought, she said, "Are you cheating on me?"

WOMAN. I like that I had a space, just one space, where I didn't have to be a Black mom or a Black Social Media director or even a Black Woman.

MAN. Sorry?

WOMAN. I could just be a girl, having perfectly average sex with a perfectly average man.

MAN. Cheating? On who. *You?*

WOMAN. But these kindsa situations aren't built to last. So after one last weekend together, I made a decision. Not to like, call it off because there was nothing to call off so I decided to, like, ghost myself out of it.

MAN. I'm not cheating on you. Why would I cheat on you? And she's like, "What about last weekend? When I was visiting my mother. You didn't have anyone here?

WOMAN. So we met at a brownstone on 127th street where he was contracted to paint a living room.

MAN. *(To us; definitively.)* I've never – and I mean *ever* – cheated on my wife. I'm faithful...*pathetically* faithful. I'm so faithful, sometimes I'll have dreams that I'm cheating on Karen. But...the weird thing is...even the girl I'm cheating with, like, *in* my dream? Is played *by* Karen. It's not her but it's her body. Her face. That's how whipped I am. I can't even cheat on my wife in my sleep.

WOMAN. Did I mention this married dude I was sleeping with was also white? I mean...he was from Moldova which I didn't even look up. I just know it's white and he's white and makes me wonder, like, what am I looking for? I'm almost forty. I've only slept with seven people in my entire life because I'm *really* picky and all of them were white.

MAN. Even though I'm faithful, the way Karen was lookin' at me in the hallway...it was like she knew something. Something I didn't. I swore she grew. I could see my reflection, like, shrink in her bright yellow eyes as she grew, uncoiling, savoring it, the moment right before the strike. Then her hand appeared from behind her back.

(Demonstrates.) Like this. Turns her fist over and opens it to reveal...the pink panties.

"So where did these come from?"

ACT TWO

WOMAN. The best part about the, uh…"affair" is a bougie word but, like, the best part about hooking up with a contractor was that he had keys to bougie apartments and he knew when they'd be gone. It was a great way to see the city.

MAN. And I was like, "Those? Those are your panties, right?" And she says, and I'll never forget this, she said. "No, these are *not* mine. *These* are way too nice."

WOMAN. The last time we hooked up was at a brownstone on 127th and Malcolm X Boulevard.

MAN. I thought they were yours! That's why I put them on – *(Catches himself.)*

WOMAN. We did it on a sofa covered in plastic.

MAN. And she says, "And that's why you put them on *what*."

WOMAN. It was hot. The plastic stuck to our sweat.

MAN. And I said "that's why I put them on…*the bed*. If they belonged to my side piece why would I put them on the bed." Then she was like, "*I* put them on the bed. After I found them under the couch. They fell out when I removed the plastic." And that's when I remembered something:

WOMAN. We were always careful not to leave anything behind. We checked for security cameras, door men, baby cams. We had a whole system.

MAN. "Baby, I wasn't here either. The painter was here. Remember? I stayed with Mike cuz the paint fumes fuck up my sinuses. I'm not cheating!"

WOMAN. In the shower, I watched flecks of paint dissolve and circle the drain. And it was then that I knew. I knew this was the last time I'd see him. I made up some reason I had to go. And I think it was at the doorway I said something vague. Vague and a little…mean? I said… "So I'll see you around."

(Beat.)

WOMAN. I'll see. You. Around.

MAN. By now we're at the doorway and she's got the panties in her hand and she's pushing them against my chest. "You're a cad," she said. Cad. She's never used the word "cad" before or since. I got this image of me driving a red sports car, smoking a cigarette against a greenscreen with the Tuscan mountains passing behind me. "You're a cad" she said "now take your panties, get the fuck out of our apartment." *Slam.*

MAN.	**WOMAN.**
So I'm walking down Malcolm X Boulevard.	So I'm walking down Malcolm X Boulevard.

MAN. ...with a stranger's panties in my pocket looking for a trash can.

WOMAN. I was on my way to get groceries when I pass the brownstone. This was about a week after we said goodbye and I stopped in front of the apartment. And I stopped for three seconds. One... two... three: And then it happened: I cried.

MAN. I'm buggin', right. I didn't shower. I could feel the COVID and the chlamydia like...wedging right up the middle of me, swishing around parts I didn't even know I had. And it's not like I haven't seen panties laying around the house before. But why these? I thought putting them on was my way of, like, feeling closer to my wife. So did I choose them because I knew on some level, some hormonal level that they were not hers. Unconsciously was I, like, wanting to feel closer to someone else? But who? Who did I get closer to?

WOMAN. I cried hard. I...I fucking *wept* because for some reason...for some stupid reason I like, missed this dumb, dusty white dude from Moldova who I wasn't even that attracted to but I like...loved him. And I wanted him to know how much I loved him. My love felt dumb. And crying made me feel dumber. So I kept walking before anyone could see me. And that's when I crossed 125th street.

MAN. I heard it before I saw it.

WOMAN. I felt it before I saw it.

WOMAN. When crazy shit goes down in the city streets, you can feel the pressure in the atmosphere drop. Everything, like, *(Breathes in deeply.)* at the same time. The trees, the sidewalk, even the sky *(Breathes in deeply.)* and for a split second there's no air, no wind. Animals disappear. And then...

MAN. *Skirrrrrrrrr...*

WOMAN. Everything exhales.

MAN. ...rrrrrrrrr – *Bang!* Like that.

WOMAN. The whole city screams at once.

MAN. By the time I got to one twenty-five, there's a crowd forming around the corner of Whole Foods.

WOMAN. A car, heading West, sped across oncoming traffic, drove up on the motherfuckin' sidewalk, and crashed right into the motherfuckin' Whole Foods.

MAN. "Charlottesville."

WOMAN. "Charlottesville."

WOMAN. It's here now.

MAN. There was a BLM march scheduled the next day and these nazis are sending a message. Tryin' to scare us by driving into a Whole Foods. To be honest, I fuckin' hate Whole Foods. But that's *our* Whole Foods, goddamnit! *Harlem's* Whole Foods. If anyone's gonna smash a car through the salad bar it's gonna be *me*!

ACT THREE

MAN. By the time I got to the scene, they were helping a woman out of the car.

WOMAN. No Nazis. Just an old woman. Not old, just… older. Spanish.

MAN. No one was hurt.

WOMAN. No one. On the busiest street in New York at a Whole Foods during lunch hour – not a single person was hurt. Not even the woman driving the car.

MAN. They asked the Spanish lady if she was hurt and she said:

WOMAN. Flamenco.

MAN. Are you drunk? And she was like:

WOMAN. Flamenco.

MAN. I saw a good-looking sistah in the crowd, arms folded, pale, shaken up, like she knew what happened.

WOMAN. I told him she lost control of her car. Then he asked me:

(They turn to address each other.)

MAN. What's she talking about flamingos for?

WOMAN. She saying *flamenco*. Like the dance.

MAN. Flamenco?

(Beat.)

Is she drunk? Crazy?

WOMAN. She's lonely.

MAN. …lonely…

WOMAN. Or maybe she just wants someone to dance with.

MAN. Are you okay?

WOMAN. No.

MAN. The paramedics/ are on the –

WOMAN. Three feet…she missed me by three feet.

MAN. Word?

WOMAN. If I didn't stop for three seconds on 127th I'd be dead.

MAN. I live on 127th.

WOMAN. Really?

MAN. What's your name?

> *(They turn back to addressing us. But they are now aware of each other's presence, building momentum off each other's lines.)*

WOMAN. That's when the Spanish lady stood up and pointed at the sky.

MAN. So we looked up at the sky.

WOMAN. And then…

MAN. I saw it.

WOMAN. We all saw it.

WOMAN. Birds.

MAN. Pink birds.

WOMAN. Flamingos.

MAN. Hundreds.

WOMAN. Thousands.

MAN. Too many flamingos.

WOMAN. They were flying, flocks and flocks of them, North, across 125th street.

MAN. I did not know there were flamingos in New York City?

WOMAN. There are no flamingos north of South Carolina. These are tropical birds. Yet...

MAN. Here they are.

WOMAN. So many the sky was pink, flamingo pink, like... I don't know, it was like –

MAN. All of New York City was stretched by taffy. No, it was more like –

WOMAN. Cotton candy. But it shimmered and moved and like, shed. It was –

MAN. Scary.

WOMAN. Beautiful.

MAN. We froze.

WOMAN. Even the paramedics froze.

MAN. And after about one...

WOMAN. ...two minutes...the flamingos...

MAN. ...as suddenly as they appeared...

WOMAN. ...were gone.

ACT FOUR

MAN. People went back to shopping an hour later.

WOMAN. By the next day, the window to Whole Foods had already been replaced.

MAN. And over the next couple months, you'd be walking around and see a pink feather on the ground.

WOMAN. For a while I'd pick them up and save them. My daughter used them to decorate her doll's hair.

MAN. My wife used them for bookmarks. Then Fall came.

WOMAN. By Fall you'd see a random dirty pink feather mixed in with the dead leaves.

MAN. They collected around the gutters…

WOMAN. Pink feathers mashed into the corner of trash cans, pipes…

WOMAN. Then Winter came.

MAN. And the snow covered them up. And when the snow melted…

WOMAN. …there were no more feathers.

   (Beat.)

MAN. It's like the whole thing never happened.

End

Goddess Help Us

by Christina Anderson

GODDESS HELP US was first presented during The New Black Fest at the Apollo Theater on April 22, 2022. The reading was directed by Goldie Patrick, with stage directions read by Lynnette Freeman. The cast was as follows:

ELLIE . . . . .Marinda Anderson
FREDI . . . . Alana Bowers
MILLS . . . . Lakisha May

CHARACTERS

ELLIE – early 30s, Black American woman. A musician, software designer.

FREDI – late 30s, Black American woman. A musician. Has a Grammy on her bookcase.

MILLS – early 30s, Black American woman. A music hobbyist. Ellie's roommate and best friend.

SETTING

Ellie's kitchen in Harlem, NY.
Fredi's kitchen somewhere else in New York.
Convention lobby.

TIME

It flows in a dream-like way. We are present in Ellie's kitchen on a weekday morning. We flow back five years in Fredi's kitchen on a Friday evening. We snap forward to a music conference in Austin. We touch various moments throughout a specific span of time.

AUTHOR'S NOTES

The "=.=" symbol is called chicken feet. Given the context of the scene, it represents an active moment that transcends words. It can be a gesture, a look, or a consideration to say the next line (or the choice to say something different). The duration of the moment should be no longer than a sneeze.

There is an unspoken intimacy between Fredi and Ellie. At times it breathes in the music. Other times it breathes in the exchanges that take place in Fredi's kitchen.

(Two cramped kitchens.)

(One in Harlem.)

(The other <u>not</u> in Harlem.)

*(**ELLIE** and **MILLS** sit in the Harlem kitchen.)*

(They stare at their phones, reading the same thing.)

(The <u>not</u>-Harlem kitchen is empty.)

(But something burns.)

(Is it the farro cooking on the stove?)

(The gluten-free bread in the toaster?)

(Or the stuffed butternut squash in the oven?)

(Whatever it is, it's definitely burning.)

(And instead of smoke, the <u>not</u>-Harlem kitchen fills with sanctimony.)

(What does sanctimony look like in this play world? Is it purple light? Bubbles? Packing peanuts?)

*(From the Harlem kitchen **ELLIE** speaks to us:)*

ELLIE. My name is Ellie.

This is my kitchen.

That's my roommate, Mills.

ELLIE. We live in Harlem.

And in this room,

at this moment,

time feels like it folds into itself.

Right now it feels like 1925, '65, '85, 2005, two thousand and twenty...

(Shift.)

Five years ago, I attended an event not far from my apartment.

A panel discussion. Four musicians talked history, future, and craft.

One of them said things that made me sit up a bit taller.

Her presence impacted me. And many others.

I introduced myself afterwards. That was five years ago.

This morning, five years later, I read an essay she just published.

It's about me. Without naming me.

It contains a litany of wrongs I supposedly committed against her –

MILLS. You have to respond.

Fill in the gaps she conveniently skipped.

ELLIE. I don't know if I want to do that.

MILLS. Why not?

The way she describes what went down

makes you look suspect.

She writes an essay; you write one back.

ELLIE. No essay.

If people want the truth, they have to look me in the eye and hear my words. I'd rather post a video.

> *(Hesitates.)*

But I don't know if I want to respond.

> *(Annoyed.)*

Why does she get to dictate how this goes, again?

She starts things, she stops things…

All I do with this woman is react –

> *(In the not-Harlem kitchen filled with sanctimony smoke, the detector goes off. But instead of the typical high-pitched beeps, we hear snippets of ELLIE's opening monologue:)*

SANCTIMONY ALARM. "…time feels like it folds into itself. Her presence impacted me…"

> *(FREDI rushes in. She opens windows, shuts off the oven, uses a dish towel to fan the sanctimony away from the detector.)*

"…It's about me. Without naming me… Five years ago… Five years ago… Five years ago"

> *(ELLIE leaves the present day of her Harlem kitchen and enters Fredi's not-Harlem kitchen from five years ago. FREDI passes her the dish towel. ELLIE continues to fan the sanctimony from the detector as FREDI tries to restore and salvage things.)*

> *(The alarm falls silent. ELLIE continues to wave the dish towel as she speaks to us:)*

ELLIE. This is Fredi.

>Who I heard speak on that panel.
>
>I introduced myself afterwards
>
>and a few weeks later I'm here.
>
>In her *not*-Harlem kitchen.
>
>She invited me over for dinner.
>
>>*(Acknowledges the disaster of the burnt meal.)*
>
>But she ended up ordering out –

FREDI. I'm sorry about this, Ellie.

ELLIE. It's okay.

FREDI. I didn't smell anything burning.

ELLIE. I didn't either.

FREDI. The alarm stopped.

>I think you can stop...

ELLIE. Oh...

>*(Stops waving the dish towel.)*
>
>What can I do?

FREDI. Relax while I order from the pizza place downstairs. What do you like on yours?

ELLIE. Whatever is fine with me.

FREDI. Veggie?

ELLIE. Yes.

>*(**FREDI** places the call. **ELLIE** speaks to us:)*
>
>Fredi is a musician who comes from a long line of family
>
>that played, wrote, painted, and danced in every major
>
>Black arts movement since the 1920s.

She feels like a Renaissance – this is the first thing I notice about her

when I'm here at her apartment. Time feels like it folds into itself.

She feels like 1925, '65, two thousand and twenty –

FREDI. *(Into the phone.)* Thanks Tony…

(Ends the call.)

They'll bring it up in a few.

ELLIE. Okay.

FREDI. So the plugin?

ELLIE. The plugin…?

FREDI. Before the detector went off, you were telling me about…

ELLIE. Oh. Right.

FREDI. Keep talking. I'm getting our glasses.

*(**FREDI** exits.)*

ELLIE. Uhhh…yea. So I'm designing this new software synth.

It's the fifth one I created from scratch.

I do everything: record the sounds, write the program, design the UI…

*(**FREDI** re-enters with their glasses. **ELLIE** takes hers.)*

FREDI. What's the new one?

ELLIE. It's in beta. I call it: Goddess Help Us…

FREDI. That is an amazing name for an instrument…

ELLIE. Thanks. I want it to have the vibe of a confidante, a friend, a guide.

ELLIE. So the sounds you can get from it will be earthy, grounded, yet ethereal.

Like good advice from a trusted friend or an ancestor.

FREDI. Give me an idea of what it sounds like.

ELLIE. Uhhh... I don't have my computer...

FREDI. Sing something.

> (**ELLIE** *is shy to do this.*)

No? Okay, well, describe one of the sounds to me and I'll try to recreate it.

> (**ELLIE** *speaks to us.*)

ELLIE. I did.

And she sang...

> (**FREDI** *sings an earthy and ethereal improvised tune. Roberta Flack meets The Weeknd...*)

I thought it was beautiful.

> (*Listens.*)

Later in the evening, Fredi asked if I'd like to

collab on a project. Create a virtual synth

from her great-grandmother's piano –

FREDI. I think we could make something really magical.

I'd play every note, conjure every sound we can imagine from it.

And you'd record it all.

The piano isn't perfect, but there's charm in that, you know?

There's history, too. Thelonius Monk played it once...

ELLIE. *(To us.)* I build software instruments.

You can download them, like an app,

and play them on your phone, laptop, tablet...

I don't charge too much. Between ten, twenty-five dollars.

Solange used one of my synths on a song...

but she never released it. The song, I mean.

    *(**MILLS** reads an excerpt from Fredi's essay:)*

MILLS. "...this person's attempt to 'cancel' me is pathetic and disappointing. I do not profess my fame. That's never been my style. But I do acknowledge my artistic status and recognition is greater than others. So I'm used to being approached by young artists. I can often sense the hunger to take but never give. I hoped this person was different. But I was wrong."

=.=

Fredi is such a trifling –

    (Fredi's doorbell rings.)

FREDI. Yay! Pizza's here.

    *(**FREDI** exits to get it.)*

ELLIE. *(To us.)* When a certain type of artist gets called out,

there's a tendency for that person to latch onto

another artist

to justify, scapegoat, or what-about the situation.

Usually, the artist who gets dragged into the situation has *less* power than the person who's being called out.

=.=

Less *social* power, that is.

ELLIE. (Because what type of power are Black artists really allowed to have?)

=.=

The artist with less power must fulfill specific needs

for any deflection or distraction to stick.

=.=

I know this.

I've *seen* this over and over.

What Fredi did, isn't about me. Not really.

She dragged me into a mess that she created herself.

I *know* this.

But the urge is overwhelming to respond

in the same public way I was dragged in.

> *(We jump in time.)*
>
> *(At a music conference.)*
>
> (**FREDI** *enters wearing a jacket, carrying a purse.*)
>
> *(She sees* **ELLIE**, *hesitates, then decides to approach.)*

FREDI. Ellie?

> (**ELLIE** *looks.*)
>
> *(Sees who it is.)*
>
> *(Says to us:)*

ELLIE. It's a year *after* Fredi published that essay.

We're at a large music conference.

I just finished speaking on a panel.

(To **FREDI**.*)* Hi, Fredi...you trifling piece of shit –

> *(An argument ensues à la* Real Housewives of Atlanta *reunion special:)*

ELLIE.
Bullshit?! You say hi to me like we all buddy, buddy –

Courteous? *(Scoffs.)* Bitch define courteous – you don't even know –

What, like the way you fucked up everything you could and tried to take me down with you.

I spent years working on that instrument.
I never got paid for any of it.

And when I tried to make a bit of money just to break even, you call me greedy, selfish, entitled. And now you sass your way to me to say "hi" –

FREDI.
Don't come at me with this bullshit.
I'm trying to be a civil human being, be courteous to your selfish ass, but –

I know better than you!
I know better than you!

You threw me under the bus the first chance you got, Ellie. User! User! That's all you are –

Sing that sanctimony song, hoe! Sing!

Stop playing the victim!
Stop playing the victim!
No one believes that shit coming from you –

(**ELLIE** *breaks away from this argument.*)

ELLIE. This clash never happened.

We *did* see each other at the music conference.

But I was on one side of a crowded room. She was on the other.

We made eye contact, but neither one of us spoke.

(**FREDI** *and* **ELLIE** *make eye contact.*)

(*A silent exchange.*)

(*From their body language it's difficult to know who feels exposed, who feels justified.*)

(**FREDI** *breaks the moment. Exits.*)

(**MILLS** *speaks from their Harlem kitchen.*)

MILLS. (*To* **ELLIE**.) I know Fredi's sister.

She works out at my gym.

We take the same Soca cardio class.

Our small talk is on the brink of becoming conversation.

(**ELLIE** *enters the kitchen.*)

(*Says to us:*)

ELLIE. I love Mills.

She's that friend that will see revenge thru to the end.

(*To* **MILLS**.) I don't want to involve family in this.

MILLS. You don't want to respond publicly.

You don't want me to trip her sister up.

What do you want?

ELLIE. Not to feel so stupid…

MILLS. You shouldn't feel stupid.

You didn't do anything wrong, Ellie.

Fredi was the one who's been saying stupid shit all along.

Not you.

> (**FREDI** *enters her kitchen with the food delivery.*)

FREDI. I got a large salad as well.

Their in-house dressing is awful, tho.

Give me a few minutes to make some from scratch.

ELLIE. *(To us.)* Fredi did an interview a few weeks before we were scheduled to release the instrument.

That interview was the beginning of the end –

> (*Mid-interview with* Vogue *or* O Magazine… *or something equally notable. She speaks at an interviewer who's seated at the fourth wall.*)

FREDI. A few haters say I coast on nepotism. But did nepotism teach me piano? Guitar? Did nepotism teach me composition? There are tons of artists who coast with absolutely no talent and they're never called out. They coast on their "identity"…and get all this praise for it. I mean, being a Black, gay, genocide survivor-of-whatever doesn't make you an artist, you know? Can you make your work without your personal narrative? That's what I want to know. I made three charting albums because I know how to make good music. Period. Do that and *maybe* I can respect you.

> (**FREDI** *goes back to making dressing.*)

ELLIE. That quote went viral.

I had already sunk fifteen hundred dollars

of my own money into *her* instrument.

Then she tweets:

FREDI. "All I was trying to say is, I just wish I could know the work BEFORE I find out about a person's trauma. When I was younger, I read (and fell in love) with Langston Hughes' poems without having to know he slept with men!"

=.= *(Returns to the moment with* **ELLIE***.)*

I put a bit of honey in this dressing is that okay? I promise it's not too sweet.

ELLIE. Yea, sure. That's fine.

(**FREDI** *smiles.*)

(Notices.) What?

FREDI. "Goddess Help Us."

That's such a great name for an instrument.

It feels like a pure and magnificent plea to the muse.

I think you and I can make something really special, Ellie.

ELLIE. Me and you?

FREDI. Yes...me and you.

ELLIE. *(To us.)* We started work on it.

My availability was determined

by hers.

I swayed with her schedule.

Things just fell into place like that.

We never discussed timeline.

She'd contact me.

FREDI. Can you come over?

ELLIE. I'd say yes.

And we'd be in her apartment.

Her seated at the piano.

Me, recording device in hand.

A tedious process that she somehow

made spiritual. There were sunrises.

Half-moons. Snow falls. Leaves changing.

Time folds into itself...

> (*A new moment from the past.*)
>
> (*An email alert chimes from* **FREDI***'s phone.*)
>
> (*She checks it.*)

FREDI. (*Reads.*) "...audio files are attached as always. There are some lovely, unexpected moments throughout..."

> (*Within this same new moment from the past,* **ELLIE** *converses with* **MILLS** *in their Harlem kitchen.*)

ELLIE. (*A bit anxious?*) I just sent Fredi an email.

MILLS. Don't you always send her an email?

You're working on the plugin...

ELLIE. Yes, but I think I feel weird about what I wrote...

FREDI. (*Reads.*) "Sound is a remarkable fusion of humanity, time, and organic elements – I remember this as I listen to these files. As I record your ancestor's instrument... I hear you as well. We haven't talked about this. But I hear you as you play. Listen for the exchanges of your presses, your pulsive breath and then...the release of a single note into the air... I think we should magnify these moments, make them a part of our instrument. I clock my reactions each time and..."

ELLIE. *(To* **MILLS**.*)* I feel weird about it, Mills.

MILLS. Why?

ELLIE. It's like I left my hair tie on her bathroom sink...

MILLS. *(Understands.)* Ohhh...innocuous, but maybe a little...

ELLIE. ...maybe a little not, yea.

MILLS. I'm sure it's fine.

Don't feel weird.

You've been working with her for months now.

Emails go back and forth.

It's fine.

FREDI. *(Reads.)* "...there is a cherished sensation here. I'm grateful for these experiences with you Fredi. I have a quiet wish to hold them but know it's selfish to do so. We must share these sounds with the world..."

> *(A few days after* **ELLIE** *sent that email, we're in* **FREDI**'s *not-Harlem kitchen. She speaks to* **ELLIE**.*)*

Ellie thank you for making it here on such short notice.

I keep promising not to do this to you...

> *(**ELLIE** leaves her kitchen, enters **FREDI**'s.)*

ELLIE. Don't worry about it, Fredi.

FREDI. My red eye to Italy got cancelled, so I have the time to squeeze in one more session before I leave in the morning.

You hungry? Thirsty? Look in the fridge.

Have whatever you want. We can order something, too.

ELLIE. I'm okay.

FREDI. How are you? How's work?

ELLIE. Good. My seniors have officially

entered the "I don't know what I'm doing"

phase of their final projects.

FREDI. *(Joke-y.)* I never left that phase...

ELLIE. I know, right?

But they're good.

Classes are good.

Teaching's good.

How about you?

Are you excited for the tour?

FREDI. I am... I have a really great group

of musicians backing me. Fun, smart, talented.

This is my... *(Counts it out.)* ...seventh tour in Europe,

but mostly first-time venues this round.

So a bit of old, a bit of new.

ELLIE. I'm sure it'll be great.

FREDI. I listened to the files you sent.

They sound great.

ELLIE. *(Nervous?)* I think so, too.

FREDI. And I agree with you...

about the sensation.

ELLIE. =.=

FREDI. You feel weird that you wrote all that, right?

(*A nervous laugh from* **ELLIE***?*)

I knew it.

As soon as I read it, I thought:

Ellie is swimming in regret soup right now.

ELLIE. I was. I am.

I felt weird. Still feel weird.

And when you didn't respond to it –

FREDI. That's my fault. I'm sorry.

My inbox is flooded with tour prep stuff.

ELLIE. Mills told me not to freak out.

FREDI. She's right.

And what you wrote is right, too.

Let's put what you hear of me

into it.

=.= (*A realization in the moment?*)

You make it easy for me to play, Ellie.

ELLIE. =.=

FREDI. I play easily, but there are only a few humans in this world

who can create the space that invites an ease within me

when I play. The fusion of humanity, time, and organic elements –

ELLIE. *(To us.)* Fredi pasted that email I wrote in her essay.

She said it captured how I was "determined to insert myself into her artmaking."

She said she chose to ignore it because she felt "uncomfortable by the subtext."

(In the Harlem kitchen.)

MILLS. Are you going to say anything to your students?

*(**FREDI** exits. **ELLIE** enters the Harlem kitchen.)*

ELLIE. *(Remembers.)* Oh god, my students.

I teach tomorrow.

MILLS. Lecture or seminar?

ELLIE. Seminar.

Seven students.

And two of them are Fredi stans.

(To us.) Within five minutes of my 10:30 a.m. class, the questions began.

But they weren't really questions, they were

accusations. Twenty-year-olds defending

the honor of a thirty-five-year-old woman

they have never met.

But they know me and I'm just their adjunct professor

who they sit with once a week.

They're convinced, without hesitation, that I'd take from her.

"Why would Fredi lie?" They ask.

"Why use her name even though you think she's homophobic?"

MILLS. You never said she was homophobic!

ELLIE. I know!

MILLS. So what'd you say to them?

ELLIE. *(To us and* **MILLS.***)* "This is a course on Aesthetics & Composition in Music Theory

within the 20th Century. Period. If you are not prepared or willing

to discuss Duke Ellington's *Black and Tan Fantasy*. You can leave this room

and we will see you next week to continue our work pre-determined by the syllabus."

=.=

Those two students walked out.

> *(We return to that initial dinner with* **FREDI** *and* **ELLIE.** **FREDI** *enters with the food delivery she ordered.)*

FREDI. I got a large salad as well.

Their in-house dressing is awful, tho.

Give me a few minutes to make some from scratch.

> *(***FREDI** *makes the salad dressing.)*

> *(***ELLIE,** *half-in/half-out of this moment from the past, speaks to* **FREDI** *who is oblivious to the following divulgence.)*

ELLIE. *(To* **FREDI***?)* I am Black. I am queer. I am an artist.

And you and I made this new instrument

with your family's narrative attached to it.

And a few weeks before we're about to release it,

you back-handedly denounce my identities,

the identities of millions of other artists like me.

You elevate your narrative while claiming the narrative of others to be a distraction...

> (**MILLS** *sits at a keyboard connected to a laptop.*)

MILLS. *(Announces.)* "Trails" a software synth conceived by Fredi Styles, created by Ellie Crawford.

> (**MILLS** *plays the instrument, accompanies the following:*)

ELLIE. And yes, I still chose to release the instrument.

$45.99, buy now.

And yes, I used your name to promote it.

Because that was the deal, remember?

I had to try and make some type of money on it.

And yes, I also posted that if I had a trust fund I could walk away

and never release this synth, but I don't, so I can't.

FREDI. *(Oblivious.)* I put a bit of honey in this recipe, is that okay? I promise it's not too sweet.

ELLIE. Yea, sure. That's fine.

> (**FREDI** *smiles.*)

(Notices.) What?

FREDI. "Goddess Help Us."

That's such a great name for an instrument.

It feels like a pure and magnificent plea to the muse.

I think you and I can make something really special, Ellie.

ELLIE. Me and you?

FREDI. Yes...me and you.

ELLIE. Okay, now I'm intrigued.

What exactly do you have in mind, Fredi Styles?

> *(**MILLS** continues to play, her composition swells into a journey that maybe captures/ recounts what **ELLIE** and **FREDI** are about to go through, have been through.)*

> *(Oblivious to the accompaniment, **ELLIE** and **FREDI** sit down to eat. There's an ease and joyfulness between the two of them as they quietly daydream what's possible with their collaboration.)*

> *(This image continues for a few moments until...)*

> *(Blackout.)*

The Moon, The Sun and The Stories We Play

A play in moments
by Dane Figueroa Edidi

THE MOON, THE SUN AND THE STORIES WE PLAY was first presented during The New Black Fest at the Apollo Theater on April 25, 2022. The reading was directed by Goldie Patrick. The cast was as follows:

SELENE . . . . Dane Figueroa Edidi
GREGORY . . . . Jeorge Watson
GRANDMOTHER . . . . Stephanie Berry

CHARACTERS

SELENE – A Black Trans Woman. A Moon Woman. An Artist.
GREGORY – A Black man (cis or trans). A Man of Sun. A producer.
GRANDMA – A Black cis woman. A Spirit. A Memory. A Storyteller.

SETTING

A New York Apartment, Haunted by the Unspoken,
Needing to Be Exorcised by the Letting Go.

TIME

Hours in A Day, Moments between feelings, A Time when Suns
are preparing to set... or Any Day after the year 2021.

AUTHOR'S NOTES

The Narrator is the Spirit of Selene's Grandmother
While the play is grounded in reality, it is not realism
The most ideal director for this play is a Black woman, the least ideal is a white cis man

Scene One

The Moon Wakes On A River Of Tears

GRANDMA. We are in a small apartment

Simple in its grandeur

Warm in its embrace

There is a small table in the corner with a cup of water

A libation of memory

There is another table

Round like always

Two chairs settled on opposite sides of it

waiting on a reason to draw themselves together

A window

With sun peering through

is behind it

(There is the beep of a machine.)

GREGORY. *(On the message machine.)* Hey babe

I hope you are doing well

So

…

I have some bad news

…

GRANDMA. A door opens somewhere

> Selene appears
>
> Sorrow hanging to her
>
>> (**SELENE** *appears, sorrow hanging to her.*)
>
> A night gown clinging to body
>
> desperately
>
> She moves towards the window
>
> A ghost in her own flesh
>
> Her steps
>
> gingerly
>
> against the ground
>
> Trying to summon something of the days before

GREGORY. *(On the message machine.)* So they want to pass on your play

> The team just feels like it really won't work in this season's slot
>
> I really did try to fight for you...

GRANDMA. Selene

> A moon woman
>
> skin that lets you know she Black
>
> and full of that old magic
>
> of memories
>
> stored there in the treasure troves of melanin
>
> The kind hidden within discovery and reclamation

GREGORY. *(On the message machine.)* I mean I kept telling you it wasn't commercial enough

I'm sorry

...

It's just

Those types of plays are hard to sell

...

I'm sorry

GRANDMA. She stands in front of the window

The sun an ocean of Gold

The blinds

Sullen

Attempting to keep it at bay

Sunlight weeps

dripping themselves down walls

dropping against flesh

glaring when they touch eye

Selene covers her eyes

Daring not to close the blinds

She

A phantom living in her tomorrows

Goes back into her room

SELENE. Can you believe this shit Grandma

GRANDMA. She shuts the door

Scene Two

The Laughter of Tears Sound Like Joy

    (**GRANDMA** *goes to the clock and turns it.*)

GRANDMA. An hour later

    An alarm blares

    Screaming

    "Get up gal

    You got magic to conjure

    You got screams to hurl

    You got white folk to rattle"

        (*She laughs.*)

        (*We hear the sounds of* **SELENE** *getting ready.*)

    The sound of a shower

    The sound of a ticking clock

    The sound of teeth being brushed

    The sound of make up being put on

    The sound of hair being brushed

    sounds

    Of mourning hidden behind each gesture

    Selene readies herself

    Lullabies of womanhood singing

    Sounds

        (**SELENE** *comes out of her room smiling.*)

    She emerges

A painting of joy

Tears hidden behind a smile

The doorbell rings

Selene sighs

The sounds of keys jiggling

The door opens

Gregory emerges bathed in artificial light

Gregory is a man of sun

Where he goes space fills with heat

The thing about heat is

too much can burn ya

Dry you out

Make you so thirsty that the great flood itself won't fill the sea in you

GREGORY. I called you

SELENE. I know

GRANDMA. Gregory looks at her

Wanting to conjure joy in her

But he ain't got the range

She knows this so her smile tries to assuage his discomfort

SELENE. Greg it's fine

I am feeling much better

I even sent my manuscript in to my publisher

A Bitch may not have Broadway

But she know how to write a novel

GREGORY. What did he say

SELENE. I just sent it to him yesterday

> *(She giggles.)*

GRANDMA. Her giggle is music

His heart dances

GREGORY. So you not going to back out of coming to brunch with me

SELENE. No

Not this time

GREGORY. Soooo you'll go with me to see a matinee of the show I produced too

SELENE. Sure

It got really great reviews and was touted as being proof Broadway was back how could I miss that

I'm proud of you

GRANDMA. Selene kisses him on the cheek

This calms him

This frustrates her

But masquerades become commonplace in a world of men

They take each other's hand and smiles cross their lips

Scene Three

To Wake the Dead One Must Know How to Shout

>(**GRANDMA** *turns the clock.*)

GRANDMA. The morning births the afternoon

>The afternoon births evening

>The apartment whispers with the thrill of silence

>The front door opens

>Laughter making love on air

>Selene and Gregory come in

SELENE. And my grandma says

>"Fuck them

>And their racist grandaddy"

GRANDMA. The door shuts

>(**GREGORY** *and* **SELENE** *laugh.*)

GREGORY. Your grandmother was wild

SELENE. Sometimes

GRANDMA. As the lights come on in the apartment

>Gregory sits down

SELENE. You want some tea

GREGORY. Sure

GRANDMA. She goes to make tea

>A shadow burning with exuberance

>She places the cups down on the table

>The tea kettle waits to boil

SELENE. So

That was the show you produced

GREGORY. What does that mean

SELENE. Mmm

It was much whiter than I thought it would be

GREGORY. Whiter

Most of the cast were BIPOC

SELENE. I am not just talking about the bodies on stage

I mean the gaze

Everything that happened was like a plea to white folks to be...

GREGORY. To Be what

SELENE. Not racist

GREGORY. Well a play should leave the audience changed

SELENE. Yes

But what audience are you most concerned with

GREGORY. Babe

You know what I mean

SELENE. You mean a white audience

Well trying to absolve them of responsibility isn't the same thing as changing them

GREGORY. There are good white people Selene

SELENE. And those "good" white people don't need to see us get raped on stage to care

GREGORY. So are we supposed to all write and produce plays that just yell at the audience for an hour and a half

SELENE. That's better than pretending that the audience has no responsibility to do better

To be better

GREGORY. Responsibility to who

SELENE. To you

To me

GRANDMA. The Tea Kettle begins to bubble

GREGORY. Girl you have a studio apartment in New York And I just produced a hit on Broadway

We ain't struggling

SELENE. But I watch the way the fear of losing everything grips you

I watch the way your throat closes up when white supremacy gets brought up in any Equity and Inclusion discussion

I see how you beg institutions to change

And do nothing when they don't

GREGORY. Why is it my job to do that

Why do I always have to give something up to make something right

I mean I don't see you turning down commissions

SELENE. And you also don't see how I'm donating to gofundmes every five seconds either

GREGORY. And how do you know I ain't

SELENE. Greg

...

Come on

GREGORY. Sometimes you have to do the thing so you can one day make the decisions

SELENE. Sometimes those days don't ever come

What good is being in the room when you hold no power

Do you know how many times I heard white folks in the media say

"Well he cast Black and Brown people as white slave masters"

And somehow

They think that's progress

Somehow

They say those words and it doesn't click just how racist

And selfish

And bigoted

That shit is

And how that's the reason why those terrorists stormed the capital on January 6th

GREGORY. Here we go again

Everything isn't that deep

SELENE. Everything is always that deep

Cause the ghosts of the past are alive

And we can either nurture them or exorcise them

GRANDMA. The Tea Kettle hisses

GREGORY. You alienate everyone with your rhetoric

SELENE. Coward

GREGORY. So

You ain't gonna break up with me

SELENE. And what does that make me

GRANDMA. In love

SELENE. Compassionate

Because I don't think you're disposable

But you make choices that make things harder for me

And for the girls who'll come after me

And I don't know if I can keep loving you how I keep loving you when you choose not to recognize that

...

Or care

GREGORY. You know I care

SELENE. But what good is your love when the whims of white men can make you abandon who you are

GREGORY. Your play was not as great as you thought it was

SELENE. Maybe not

But it was certainly necessary

GREGORY. For who Selene

Your ego

SELENE. The people you keep forgetting

GRANDMA. The Tea Kettle screams

Selene stands

Grabs the cups with the swiftness of a knife's edge

And pours the water into them

GREGORY. You just had to write something that would make people feel good

That's all

SELENE. Some of us spend our lives making people feel good

While we sit in our fear

And rage against terror

And hope that maybe today the world will fucking change

And that the land won't burn to ash

And that another Black Trans person won't be found in a gutter

And that our joy can be more than a passing friend

Some of us generate so much joy for everyone else we forget we deserve some for ourselves

I watched my grandmother do this

Being everything

To everybody

All the time

And I refuse

I refuse to become a caricature of myself

And

Sometimes

Sometimes I want to

scream

Sometimes I want to cry

And all I was doing was sitting here and begging

Pleading with you to let me tell my story

Mine

My way

But y'all don't want a Black Trans woman dictating terms and conditions

Y'all want to be saviors

Because that makes you feel less responsible

Less guilty

While y'all keep being standard bearers for classism

And patriarchy

And revised history

Where shows like to pretend the "founding fathers" were your hip-hop cousins

As opposed to the men whose terror keeps coming back to haunt this country

This planet

These worlds

I wanted to write an ancestor story

Where we can see ourselves

And hold each other

And love one another

And tell the fucking truth for once

Not for their comfort but for our fucking own

And yes screaming

And yelling

And telling white supremacy and its stewards they ain't shit

Brings me comfort

Because then the tears I shed when I am lying alone

Tears for myself

SELENE. For my sisters

For my grandma

And even for you won't always be ones of sorrow

So yes while my play made y'all uncomfortable it made me feel fucking fantastic

And you do not get to equate your discomfort with the merit of my work

GREGORY. Love...

GRANDMA. She places down the cups

Gingerly even though her words were war

She doesn't believe he is the enemy

She simply believes he is much of the same

And that makes her tired

Gregory does not speak

Something in him saying something to him

But he's been so long away from himself the language is hard to decipher

Selene

A moon Woman

Cloaked in the still of the little bit of silvery light that comes through the window

Stands and goes into the room

Gregory takes another breath

Taking off his shoes and placing them at the door

Taking off his clothes

Folding them and leaving them on the chair which he tries to move closer to the other but can not

Shirtless

Gregory

A man of the Sun

exits into the room

Ghosts stirring in their flesh

Trying to breathe each other back to life

And failing to do so

Again

And again

And again

End of Play

Holding

by Zora Howard

HOLDING was first presented during The New Black Fest at the Apollo Theater on April 25, 2022. The reading was directed by Goldie Patrick, with stage directions read by Stephanie Berry. The cast was as follows:

MARIAMA . . . . Naomi Lorrain
OPERATOR . . . . Marinda Anderson

CHARACTERS

MARIAMA – (f), Black, 30s
OPERATOR – (f), one actor will voice all

SETTING

A room.

TIME

Now.

AUTHOR'S NOTES

A speech usually follows the one immediately before it, except when one character starts speaking before the other has finished, the point of interruption is marked "/".

OPERATOR. Gracias por/ llamar a Dynamic Solutions. Escuche atentamente–

MARIAMA. *(Offstage.)* No, no, no.

English. English.

(A room, empty except for a single, wooden chair. Water leaks from several spots in the ceiling. A symphony of syncopated dripping.)

OPERATOR. *(On speakerphone.)* ...for English, press one. Para Español, oprime dos.

(A cellphone touchpad key – "beep.")

MARIAMA. *(Offstage.)* Fuck.

OPERATOR. Gracias por/ llamar a Dynamic Solutions. Escuche atentamente –

MARIAMA. *(Offstage.)* No, no, no.

English. English.

(Several keys on the touchpad at once – "beep beep beep.")

OPERATOR. Lo siento, esa/ no es una entrada válida. *(Pause.)* Gracias por llamar –

MARIAMA. *(Offstage.)* Please. Go back. English. Inglés.

(Pause. Robot sounds.)

OPERATOR. Thank you for calling Dynamic Solutions.

*(**MARIAMA** enters laden with a number of pots, some towels, and a mop, her cell phone balancing delicately on top of it all.)*

Please listen carefully to the following options as our menu has changed.

If you have an existing account, please press one.

MARIAMA. Operator.

OPERATOR. For our contractor associate line, please press two.

MARIAMA. Operator.

OPERATOR. For claims and appeals, please press three.

MARIAMA. O-per-a-tor. I would like to speak to an operator.

(*Robot sounds.*)

OPERATOR. I understand that you would like to speak to an operator. In a few words, please tell me what you're calling about.

MARIAMA. I have a leak.

OPERATOR. I'm sorry, I didn't catch that. In a few words/, please tell me what you're calling about.

MARIAMA. Leak. Leak. Water is falling from the ceiling.

OPERATOR. You can say make a payment, or press one. Existing order, or press two. Technical support, or press three. Location and hours, or press four.	**MARIAMA.** (*Receiver very close to her mouth.*) I have a leak. There is water. Falling. From my ceiling. I need someone to help me stop the water falling from –

MARIAMA. (*Losing it.*) I have a leak I have a leak I have a –

(*Pause.*)

OPERATOR. Okay. You said Liens. Is that correct?

MARIAMA. No. I said –

OPERATOR. Transferring you to our next available agent.

(*On hold now: pleasant, nondescript music fills the space.* An endless loop.* **MARIAMA** *rests a moment in the chair as she waits.*)

---

* A license to produce *HOLDING* does not include a performance license for any third-party or copyrighted music. Licensees should create an original composition or use music in the public domain. For further information, please see the Music and Third-Party Materials Use Note on page iii.

In order to better assist you, please have your thirty-six digit account number ready.

> *(Seconds haven't passed before **MARIAMA** notices a new leak on the opposite side of the room.)*

MARIAMA. What the –

> *(**MARIAMA** drags the chair across the room to get a better look.)*

OPERATOR. All of our representatives are assisting other callers. Your estimated wait time is *(Another voice.)* [two hours and fifty-three minutes].

MARIAMA. *(Re the leak.)* Where is it coming from?

OPERATOR. Rather than wait on hold, we can call you back when it's your turn within *(Another voice.)* [three hours and sixty-four minutes]. To receive a callback, say callback or press one. To remain on hold, say hold/ or press two.

MARIAMA. Hold. Hold, hold, HOLD.

> *(**MARIAMA**, now atop the chair on her tippy toes, reaches to touch the source of the most recent leak when all of a sudden an even newer [and more aggressive] leak starts up in another corner.)*

No no. No. NO!

OPERATOR. Please note, by speaking to a representative and providing personal information, you are agreeing to our privacy policy, which you may or may not find on our website.

> *(**MARIAMA** jumps down from the chair and, with a running start, slides a pot from one of the original leaks towards the new leak, nearly busting her ass in the process.)*

MARIAMA. You will not win.

> *(A success! And yet, somehow, in that moment, all of the original leaks shift about an inch and a half outside their respective pots at the same time, rendering her initial pot system obsolete.)*

Arghhhhhhhh!

OPERATOR. Your call is important to us. Please wait for the next available agent.

> *(**MARIAMA** rushes around the room like a madwoman, rearranging the pots, sliding the towels into new positions, leaping over the newly-formed puddles in between.)*

> *(A new sound is now introduced into the space. Whatever it is, it's coming from above. The leaks rebel – it is now practically raining in the room.)*

MARIAMA. *(Calling through the ceiling to the apartment upstairs.)* HELLO! HELLO YOU ARE LEAKING ON ME

> *(**MARIAMA** shoots across the space and grabs the mop. Then hops back atop the chair and starts banging on the ceiling.)*

YOU ARE LEAKING ON ME! HELLO

OPERATOR. *(Heavy southern accent.)* Hello, thank you for calling Dynamic Solutions. My name is Jessica. Who do I have/ the pleasure of –

MARIAMA. *(Still to the apartment upstairs.)* STOP PLEASE YOU ARE LEAKING ON ME!

OPERATOR. I'm sorry?

MARIAMA. YOU ARE LEAKING ON ME!

OPERATOR. Hello, is anyone there?

> (**MARIAMA**, *all of a sudden aware of the live agent on the line, dashes over to her phone.*)

MARIAMA. *(Out of breath.)* Hello?! Yes! YES. I'm here. I'm here I'm here/ I'm

OPERATOR. Thank you for calling Dynamic Solutions. This is Jessica. And whom do I have the pleasure of speaking with today?

MARIAMA. *(Still out of breath.)* Mariama. I am Mariama.

OPERATOR. How can I help you today, Mariama?

MARIAMA. I have a leak. I have many leaks. I am leaking. Everywhere.

OPERATOR. Hmmm. Well, that's no fun.

MARIAMA. *(Wtf?)* No. It is not.

OPERATOR. Let me see what I can do about that.

MARIAMA. Thank/ you.

OPERATOR. So, when you're ready, I'll just take that thirty-six digit account number from you.

MARIAMA. I don't want – I don't have that.

OPERATOR. That's okay. It's either gonna be on your membership card, or if you don't have that, you can find it right up there in the left hand corner of your last statement. You can also find it on your online account.

MARIAMA. I don't have an online account.

OPERATOR. That's no problem. I can go ahead and set that up for you –

MARIAMA. *(Exasperated.)* Is there any other way I/ can –

OPERATOR. How about, okay, let me see. What's your date of birth?

MARIAMA. May 4, 1992.

OPERATOR. ...4th, 92. Oh! Happy early birthday.

MARIAMA. Thank you.

OPERATOR. Any special plans?

MARIAMA. Umm, no.

OPERATOR. Well, that's no fun.

MARIAMA. *(???)* It's/ fine –

OPERATOR. And when you're ready, I'll just take the last four digits of your social security number?

MARIAMA. 4609.

OPERATOR. ...09. And now the last four digits of your driver's license?

MARIAMA. Ummm, 959/4

OPERATOR. And can you just verify your address for me?

MARIAMA. 296 Hamilton Place, New York/, NY –

OPERATOR. Thank you. And your blood type?

MARIAMA. I'm sorry, how is this/ relevant –

OPERATOR. That's alright. And, I see you are an organ donor in the state of Colorado, would you like to make a donation to Donate Life America?

MARIAMA. No, I'd like to –

OPERATOR. How about the Miracle Foundation?

MARIAMA. Excuse/ me?

OPERATOR. Black Lives/ Matter?

MARIAMA. *(Firm.)* No, I do not want to donate to Black Lives Matter. I just want to –

OPERATOR. *(Judgmental.)* Mmm.

MARIAMA. What's that?

OPERATOR. Okay, Mariama, I was able to get your account pulled up here. How may I assist you?

MARIAMA. *(What??)* My leak? I said I have a leak. I have several leaks. It is leaking on my head. It is leaking from everywhere and I cannot get it to stop.

OPERATOR. And how long has it been leaking on your head, ma'am?

MARIAMA. Since yesterday. Or today. I don't know when it started. It hasn't rained. Has it been raining outside?

OPERATOR. Umm –

MARIAMA. I thought it was cold. I thought it was sunny. I didn't think it rained. Or not substantially. Not enough to cause all of this. I don't know if it's the plumbing or the roof. They said I'd have to get to that eventually/,

OPERATOR. Ma'am...?

MARIAMA. that the bones were crumbling. Or the infrastructure was falling apart, that it wasn't built to last all this time. That this is to be expected. I just didn't think it would ever happen. Not like this. And not so soon. It'd been holding up just fine and then *boom*. One day. A leak. Two leaks. Seven leaks. How many leaks I cannot count. And another has just begun. I don't understand the source. Is it the pipes? Everything I do to stop it – nothing stops it. I've turned off everything, I've drained everything. I've looked for clogs, for blockages, but everything seems to be working and in good order. As far as I can see. Everything in good order. I'm in good order. Am I in good order? Everything else is working, you understand. I work. I'm working. I get up. I am where I am expected to be, except I spill. A small puddle wherever I stand. I don't know if others notice it. I'm worried others will start to complain. My neighbors. My friends. That I'm pouring over into their spaces, everything I'm holding quietly spreading beyond my reach, leaving little messes, little stains when I walk, when I come for coffee. I can hear it. Always something rushing, rushing towards me and the way it sounds coming you'd think the whole of everything would split open and bleed out until there was – but no. Just a little sliver of water. A small leak. Many small leaks. I thought I had more time.

(Pause.)

That's it.

(A long beat.)

OPERATOR. Hmm. That sounds...tough.

MARIAMA. It is.

OPERATOR. Well. I'm sure we can get that squared away for you.

MARIAMA. You can?

OPERATOR. Of course, ma'am. We're here to help.

MARIAMA. *(Such relief.)* Oh God. Oh, thank you. Thank you/, I–

OPERATOR. I'll just have to place you on a brief hold/ while I get you over to the supervisor line.

MARIAMA. No.

OPERATOR. It'll only take a couple of minutes.

MARIAMA. Please no.

OPERATOR. Before I do, is there anything else I can help you with today?

MARIAMA. Please don't go.

OPERATOR. If there isn't anything else, like I said, my name is Jessica and/ it has been my absolute pleasure to serve you.

MARIAMA. Don't go don't go don't –

OPERATOR. If you are able to stay on the line after the call for a brief survey on my performance today, I'd really appreciate it.

MARIAMA. please

OPERATOR. Transferring you over now. Hang tight.

(Automated voice.)

Your current wait time is [four hours and 55.5 seconds].

(Back on hold: endless loop music resumes.*
MARIAMA, *spent, slides to the floor, no matter the puddles around her. She closes her eyes.)*

We now offer a fast and convenient messaging experience to connect with us. A semi-live agent can message you to assist with all of your needs. If you'd like to try this service, press one. Or you can say no way José.

MARIAMA. *(Defeated.)* No way José

OPERATOR. I'm sorry I didn't –

MARIAMA. Leave me.

(After a while, the upstairs sound will start again. And then: the leaks again. All of them together this time – orchestral.)

(MARIAMA *can't move.)*

(Almost a whisper.) I have a leak. I have a leak. I have a –

I can't get it to/

---

* A license to produce *HOLDING* does not include a performance license for any third-party or copyrighted music. Licensees should create an original composition or use music in the public domain. For further information, please see the Music and Third-Party Materials Use Note on page iii.

OPERATOR. Your call is important to us. Please stay on the line for the next available representative.

> (**MARIAMA** *cries quietly to herself. She touches her cheeks to be sure of the source.*)

End of Play

www.ingramcontent.com/pod-product-compliance
Lightning Source LLC
Chambersburg PA
CBHW072008290426
44109CB00018B/2170